UNDER... YOUR RELIGION

7 MAJOR DOCTRINES THAT DEFINE **CHRISTIANITY**

MIKE MAZZALONGO

Copyright © 2016 by Mike Mazzalongo

ISBN: 978-0692584422

BibleTalk Books
14998 E. Reno
Choctaw, Oklahoma 73020

Scripture quotations taken from the New American Standard Bible®, Copyright © 1960, 1962, 1963, 1968, 1971, 1972, 1973, 1975, 1977, 1995 by The Lockman Foundation Used by permission. (www.Lockman.org)

Pages 136, 137, 154, 155, 184
187, 202, 213, 215, 216,
218, 221, 222, 225, 245,
259, 260, 263, 264, 265
266, 267, 272.
122,
(225)

TABLE OF CONTENTS

MAJOR CHRISTIAN DOCTRINES (cont'd)

VI. The Kingdom of God

VII. The Second Coming

INTRODUCTION: WHY STUDY DOCTRINE?

The reason we do and say the things we do and say as Christians is because we believe as true certain teachings (doctrines) concerning our faith. For example:

- How we worship God.

- How we feel about death and life after death.

- What motivates our effort to control our various human impulses, etc.

These are based squarely on the instructions or "doctrines" we believe come from God contained in the Bible. Many times, however, we tend to deal more with the end result (actions/habits/attitudes) created by doctrine than the actual doctrine itself.

This book was written in order to examine the reasons we, as Christians, live as we do by studying seven major doctrines upon which our faith and practice are built.

Before we begin to examine these doctrines, however, I would like to mention several reasons why such a study is important.

Jesus Commanded It

> [19] Go therefore and make disciples of all the nations, baptizing them in the name of the Father and the Son and the Holy Spirit, [20] teaching them to observe all that I commanded you; and lo, I am with you always, even to the end of the age.
> - Matthew 28:19-20

Jesus says that part of the process of making disciples is to teach them the words of Christ and encourage them to obey them. We study the doctrines of the Bible to understand God's purpose in sending Christ and Christ's purpose in sending the Apostles. Major Christian doctrine is another way of saying, "the teachings of Christ."

There is Much False Teaching

There were many early warnings that the method Satan would use to destroy the church and the faith of many was through the teaching of false doctrine.

> [17] Now I urge you, brethren, keep your eye on those who cause dissensions and hindrances contrary to the teaching which you learned, and turn away from them. [18] For such men are slaves, not of our Lord Christ but of their own appetites; and by their smooth and flattering speech they deceive the hearts of the unsuspecting.
> - Romans 16:17-18

There were many who purposefully taught false things to confuse or trap the brethren. How are we to "test" if we do not know?

> Beloved, do not believe every spirit, but test the spirits to see whether they are from God, because many false prophets have gone out into the world.
> - I John 4:1

Test the spirits.

> For the time will come when they will not endure sound doctrine; but *wanting* to have their ears tickled, they will accumulate for themselves teachers in accordance to their own desires
> - II Timothy 4:3

People often want to hear what pleases them, instead of the truth.

> [16] But avoid worldly and empty chatter, for it will lead to further ungodliness, [17] and their talk will spread like gangrene. Among them are Hymenaeus and Philetus, [18] men who have gone astray from the truth saying that the resurrection has already taken place, and they upset the faith of some.
> - II Timothy 2:16-18

False teachers spread false information about existing facts in order to produce confusion.

> [28] Be on guard for yourselves and for all the flock, among which the Holy Spirit has made you overseers, to shepherd the church of God which

9

He purchased with His own blood. [29] I know that after my departure savage wolves will come in among you, not sparing the flock; [30] and from among your own selves men will arise, speaking perverse things, to draw away the disciples after them.
- Acts 20:28-30

Even church leaders will be guilty of this sin, by ignorance or malice.

We need to study doctrine so we can know the difference between correct doctrine and false doctrine. Jesus said that the best way to examine teaching is to compare it to His own words because it will be His word that will judge in the end.

He who rejects Me and does not receive My sayings, has one who judges him; the word I spoke is what will judge him at the last day.
- John 12:48

False Doctrine Causes Problems

It divided the church

[3] If anyone advocates a different doctrine and does not agree with sound words, those of our Lord Jesus Christ, and with the doctrine conforming to godliness, [4] he is conceited and understands nothing; but he has a morbid interest in controversial questions and disputes about words, out of which arise envy, strife, abusive language, evil suspicions, [5] and constant friction between men of depraved mind and deprived of

✓

the truth, who suppose that godliness is a means of gain.
- I Timothy 6:3-5

People will align with different teachers and there will be ✓ fighting among the brethren over false teaching

It makes prisoners of false ideas

But it was because of the false brethren secretly brought in, who had sneaked in to spy out our liberty which we have in Christ Jesus, in order to bring us into bondage.
- Galatians 2:4

See to it that no one takes you captive through philosophy and empty deception, according to the tradition of men, according to the elementary principles of the world, rather than according to Christ.
- Colossians 2:8

[6] For among them are those who enter into households and captivate weak women weighed down with sins, led on by various impulses, [7] always learning and never able to come to the knowledge of the truth.
- II Timothy 3:6-7

In each instance Paul refers to Christians who are made slaves of some form of religious tradition, authority or practice that is based on false teaching, and whose only purpose is to enslave those Christians who may not know the truth. Knowing the truth, knowing correct doctrine makes you free and protects the church from division caused by false teachers.

Results of Correct Doctrine

There are not only negative reasons for studying doctrine, there are also great benefits that come from knowing the major doctrines of the Bible.

Correct doctrine leads to salvation

[14] You, however, continue in the things you have learned and become convinced of, knowing from whom you have learned them, [15] and that from childhood you have known the sacred writings which are able to give you the wisdom that leads to salvation through faith which is in Christ Jesus.
- II Timothy 3:14-15

You cannot be saved properly without knowing the true and correct doctrine about salvation.

Equips one to serve God

[16] All Scripture is inspired by God and profitable for teaching, for reproof, for correction, for training in righteousness; [17] so that the man of God may be adequate, equipped for every good work.
- II Timothy 3:16-17

We are saved so we can serve the living God, and correct doctrine teaches us how to please and serve Him.

Transforms us into the image of Christ

> But the goal of our instruction is love from a pure heart and a good conscience and a sincere faith.
> - I Timothy 1:5

Knowing the words of Christ and sowing them correctly into our hearts will produce a Christ-like heart, a Christian character, a change that will honor God and provide true witness to others. Without true doctrine we cannot know God, come to Christ or be sure of our salvation.

Outline of this book

There are many instructions or "doctrines" that the Bible teaches, but the title of this book is "*Understanding Your Religion: Seven Major Doctrines that Define Christianity*", so I have tried to select the doctrines that best represent the entire instruction given in the Bible. In other words, these are the doctrines that cover the Bible from start to finish and into which other doctrines fit.

There are seven:

I.   Doctrine of Inspiration of the Bible

II. Doctrine of the Deity of Christ

III. Doctrine of Original Goodness

IV. Doctrine of the Fall of Man

V.   Doctrine of Restoration

VI.   Doctrine of the Kingdom

VII.   Doctrine of the Second Coming

If you are familiar with these doctrines, you will be familiar with the sub-teachings that are generated by these, and you will be much more knowledgeable about why and how you are to practice the Christian faith.

MAJOR CHRISTIAN DOCTRINES

I. Inspiration of the Bible

CHAPTER 1
THE WRITING OF THE BIBLE

I want to begin by stating the fact that there is no
doctrine of the existence of God contained in the Bible.
Oh yes, people debate this in various ways but there is
no body of doctrine to provide proof and reasons to
believe in the existence of a supreme being in the Bible.

The reason for this is that the Bible assumes from the
beginning that God exists; it says so from the very first
sentence,

> In the beginning, God created the heavens and
> the earth.
> - Genesis 1:1

The Bible states this as fact and does not provide
philosophical or theological arguments to prove it.

There are ways and systems of arguments that serve to prove the existence of a higher being, an all-powerful God (apologetics), but this is not the focus of our study. We are examining the actual doctrines or teachings that are specifically contained in the Bible. A thorough knowledge of these will help us know in more detail the character, the work and the will of God, but not whether He exists or not. This we accept as true from the start.

In this context it is natural to begin with a basic doctrine that is contained in the Bible, and that is its inspiration. What does the Bible teach about itself? What is it about the Bible that makes it unique and separate from all other books? We believe the Bible teaches that it is unique and authoritative because it is directly inspired by God.

Since the Bible is a book, we need to examine the history of writing and book making before looking at the issue of inspiration.

History of Writing

Many people believed for a long time that early man was ignorant and rejected the idea that ancient civilizations used writing or writing materials. This was their main argument against the authorship of Moses or Abraham who lived thousands of years before Christ ("It could not have been Moses who wrote the first five books of the Bible because writing did not exist back then"). However, we have learned several things about ancient writing and authors since that time:

- Egypt has inscriptions that date as far back as +3000 BC.

- King Sargon I (2350 BC) has inscriptions referring to him.

- They have found letters written by Palestinian officials dating back to 1500 BC, Moses' time.

As I said before, many discounted Moses as being the author of the first five books of the Bible because he lived too early for writing to have existed, however, modern findings have confirmed writing in early civilizations and the claim that the Bible makes that Moses wrote the beginning part of the Bible has been justified. The more research, the more discoveries, the stronger the case for the Bible as the infallible Word of God.

History of Writing Materials Used in Making Ancient Books

Stone

The earliest writing materials were stone. The ten commandments (1500 BC) were inscribed on stone tablets which matches archaeological discoveries of that era.

Clay

Assyria/Babylonia used this as their main writing materials. Large libraries containing clay tablets of that period have been discovered in modern times. Ezekiel 4:1 (600 BC), God tells Ezekiel to write on a brick or clay tablet.

Wood

Wooden tableaus were used during this time as well; Isaiah 30:8 (750 BC).

Leather

Specially treated animal skins were marked upon using knives. II Timothy 4:13 probably refers to Old Testament portions written on animal skins (parchments).

Papyrus

Great advances were made as the Egyptians developed papyrus as a writing surface. Papyrus was a plant that grew along the Nile, inside was a spongy material. This material was removed and cut into strips which were laid side by side to form a sheet, another layer was then laid crosswise on top of it and both were pressed together. They were then dried and ready for use.

Sometimes a sheet was used alone for a letter or business receipt, sometimes they were attached together to form a scroll. A scroll was at times as long as thirty feet and usually nine to ten inches wide. Writing was done on one side and a wooden roll-pin was inserted for easy use. These were the "books" of the ancient world, referred to as scrolls. Leather was used in the Old Testament and with time papyrus was used in the New.

> **Papyrus codex** - Codex manuscript was used in the first and second century. These were merely single papyrus sheets put together in book form, rather than rolled. Early New Testament writings were mainly in the codex form.

Vellum codex - This development was important because most New Testament manuscripts from the 4th to the 14th century were written on this type of material.

In the late first century a king named Eumenes II of Pergamum (Asia Minor) wanted to build a world-class library. The king of Egypt, for some reason, tried to prevent this by cutting off his papyrus supply. This forced the king to develop newer forms of writing materials; he did this by improving the process of treating animal skins (which had been used for hundreds of years already). He dried and processed these by rubbing them with smooth stones. Both calf (vellum/veal) or antelope skins were used. The main value of this new process, aside from beauty as some were dyed purple and written on with gold ink, was that they lasted much longer. Papyrus tended to dry and deteriorate quickly.

Two of the most valuable copies of New Testament manuscripts that still exist today were written on vellum (veal) codex (book).

Paper

Paper was invented in the Orient in the thirteenth and fourteenth centuries and spread westward.

Printing press

Moveable type and the printing press were invented in 1448 by Guttenberg; and the first book printed on the first press was, of course, the Bible, now on display at the museum in Frankfurt, Germany. (Unfortunately Guttenberg's bankers seized his equipment and he died in debtors' prison.)

Communication age

Printing remained the main communication technique for centuries, but with time electronic communication has become predominant (telegraph, telephone, radio, television, internet, voice recognition, etc.).

In our study of writing and ancient writing materials we need to realize that when it comes to the Bible, God did not always communicate with man through the written word. In other words, God's communication with man pre-dates writing. In the beginning God communicated with man orally (Adam, Genesis 1:28; Noah, Genesis 6:13; Abraham, Genesis 17:1). Only later did God instruct Moses to begin recording His instructions.

The story of the recording of the Bible as a written record is the story of God's communication to man.

The Origin of the Bible

The word Bible comes from the Greek word "*biblia*," which means books. The complete Bible/books numbers 66 (39 in the Old Testament, and 27 in the New Testament). To study Bible origin, we must begin with the Old Testament, or a better word would be Old Covenant (alliance). This term is very useful because it helps us understand what the Bible is: the details of two covenants or agreements (accords) between God and man. The old one and the new one which replaces the old, like a lease for renting a house where certain changes are made when renewing.

The Old Testament origin

Our study of the Bible requires us to understand several features (characteristics) of the Old Testament. Written in the Hebrew language, which is still used today in Israel.

The first man charged with actually recording events and communication from God was Moses (1500 BC) (Words of covenant at Sinai, Exodus 24:1-4; Ten Commandments, Exodus 34:27:28.) Moses is credited with writing and organizing the first five books of the Bible, the Pentateuch (John 8:31). Jesus confirms this in John 7:19,

> "Did not Moses give you the Law, and yet none of you carries out the Law? Why do you seek to kill Me?"

Once God began to use human beings to record His words, this system continued after Moses. Joshua was the next writer (Joshua 24:26). Prophets recorded their history and prophecies after Joshua (Nehemiah 8:18). In this way over a period of 1500 years approximately, 28 writers completed the 39 books of the Old Testament. Malachi was the last to record in 516 BC. There were no other prophets or inspired writers until John the Baptist arrived and the Apostles began writing about Jesus' life and ministry.

All these books were collected and assembled together into one volume by 400 BC, and the Jews had a complete "Bible" 300 years before Christ.

Old Testament organization

The Jews had the same Old Testament as we do, but they organized it a little differently. They divided the Old Testament into three main sections:

1. **The Law:**

   - Pentateuch (Genesis to Deuteronomy). This was of the highest importance.

2. **The Prophets**

   - Former Prophets (Joshua, Judges, Samuel). Each had their own volume.

   - Latter Prophets: Isaiah, Jeremiah, Lamentations, Ezekiel, Minor Prophets (book of twelve in one volume).

3. **The (Holy) Writings**

   - Poetry/History (Job, Psalms, Proverbs, etc. Esther to Nehemiah, Daniel: historical).

They organized these in 24 books instead of our usual 39 books:

1. **Pentateuch:**

   - Genesis to Deuteronomy (five books).

2. **Prophets:**

   - Former (Joshua, Judges, Samuel, Kings) (four books).

   - Latter (Isaiah, Jeremiah, Ezekiel, 12 minor) (four books)

3. **Writings:**

   - Poetry/History (eleven books - 24 total)

Today we have the same books but they are divided differently:

1. **Pentateuch:**

   • Genesis to Deuteronomy (five books)

2. **History:**

   • Joshua to Esther (twelve books)

3. **Poetry:**

   • Job to Song of Solomon (five books)

4. **Major Prophets:**

   • Isaiah to Daniel (five long books)

5. **Minor Prophets:**

   • Hosea to Malachi (12 short books)

   • Total 39 books

In addition to these inspired books, the Jews wrote and circulated other books that were about the Bible but not inspired by God:

1. **The Talmud:**

   • Not to be confused with the Torah, which means law or the Law.

   • The Talmud was a body of Jewish wittings that interpreted the Old Testament.

- It contained commentaries on the Old Testament called Mishnah, and the Midrash, as well as many legal and social writings about Jewish life and religious practice.

- It was not inspired but eventually the Jews came to follow its instructions more carefully than the original Old Testament.

2. Apocryphal (Hidden Writings):

- Non-inspired religious books (Esdras, Judith, Maccabees). Many end-of-time ideas come from these.

3. Josephus:

- A history book and commentary on Jewish life during the time of Christ.

When we read the Old Testament however, we are reading the same books that the Jews read, and that Jesus and the Apostles read and taught from.

Also, these were the books that the Apostles used to proclaim the coming of Christ.

CHAPTER 2
THE NEW TESTAMENT RECORD

Many books were written about the life of Jesus, and several books were written by the Apostles and their disciples. How did they decide which books actually belonged in the New Testament?

The books that make up the New Testament are called the canon, from a Greek word which means "measuring rod." This term referred to the things that measured up when examined. In other words, when the church examined all the material that was written about Jesus, how did it decide which books belonged in the New Testament canon? There were three main factors that led the early church to form the New Testament canon and preserve it in a single compilation of 27 books.

During the time of the Apostles, the church did not have a high regard for keeping the letters that the Apostles and their disciples wrote. The Apostles were alive and producing many letters, so there was no urgency in preserving them. The prevailing thought was that Jesus was coming back in their lifetimes, so the need for preserving the material for the future was not there.

However, certain events took place that required them to begin collecting and preserving the teachings of the Lord and His Apostles for the current and future generations. Some of these events included:

The Canon of Marcion (140 AD)

Marcion was a false teacher who rejected the entire Old Testament, accepted only ten of the epistles of Paul and a part of Luke's gospel, but rejected others. He began circulating these as the official canon and so the early church was forced to decide which of the writings were authoritative, and collect and circulate these. This was done in 170 AD.

Persecution

Under the Roman Emperor Diocletian, it was a capital offense to possess a copy of the Christian scriptures. This forced the Christians of that time to choose which of these documents were worth dying for. Many uninspired and historical books were burned and only the most precious, most accepted works were kept.

Codex form

Codex is the term used to describe the "book" form where several pages were bound together instead of being attached together to form a scroll. When the codex form became popular, church leaders needed to decide which books should be grouped together into one volume. This motivated them to keep only the books that were acceptable in a single unit.

The main question for the early church was, "Which are the inspired books?" There was no meeting where they reviewed all the material and then made a decision as to which made it in and which did not. On the contrary, the early church simply accepted those works that had already been recognized as inspired over the centuries, but had not yet been collected and organized into one set. This was finally done in 367 AD and the 27 books we now have in the New Testament were confirmed into the canon by the Council of Carthage later in that century, and have remained the same since.

As the early church collected the books that would be included in the official New Testament canon it was guided by several key principles:

Authorship

If a man was inspired when he spoke, then his writings were also considered inspired. For this reason, the writings of the Apostles were quickly accepted into the canon. In addition to these, the men associated with the Apostles were also accepted. For example, Luke was accepted because of his association with the Apostle Paul, Mark because of his association with the Apostle Peter, and James was called a brother of the Lord and an Apostle (Galatians 1:19). This, of course, allowed the gospels, the letters of Paul, Peter, James and John to be natural selections for the canon.

Value of book

In some cases a book had a name attached to it but did not read like an inspired work. Many uninspired authors tried to gain an audience by putting the name of an Apostle as the author of their books. One example of this was a book entitled, "Acts of Peter" that was not actually written by the Apostle Peter and thus excluded from the canon.

Scholars tell us that it was fairly easy to distinguish between inspired and fraudulent works when you actually read the material. For example, in the "Gospel of Thomas", the author explained that Jesus made sparrows out of mud, was rebuked for doing this on the Sabbath and said, "Rise up and fly away", and the birds came to life and flew away. There is another story where He miraculously lengthened a board to fit properly while working with His earthly father Joseph.

In other words, when comparing writings, it was easy to tell the real from the fakes. The inspired books had harmony of thought, purpose and style. They had no contradictions and were accurate historically as well as theologically.

Circulation

The church did not decide which books and letters were suitable and which were not, they merely confirmed and collected the ones that had traditionally been accepted by all the churches but had never been organized into one volume before.

No new book was introduced, only those letters and volumes that had a wide circulation and acceptance after long ages of study and review. The canon was confirmed 300 years after the first writings began to be circulated.

We also believe that God was guiding and protecting the process in which His Word was recorded and preserved.

Division of the New Testament

When the canon was finally completed, the 27 books it contained were divided into the following groups:

1. Gospels:

    • Matthew, Mark, Luke and John

2. History:

    • Acts

3. Pauline Epistles:

    • Romans, I and II Corinthians, Galatians, Ephesians, Philippians, Colossians, I and II Thessalonians, I and II Timothy, Titus and Philemon

4. General Epistles:

    • Hebrews, James, I and II Peter, I, II and III John, and Jude

5. Prophecy:

    • Revelation

Most were written by Apostles or the disciples of Apostles. A couple (Hebrews and Jude) may have uncertain origins (some say Hebrews was written by Paul, Jude, Apollos or by the brother of Jesus), but they were widely accepted, and their material was perfectly in tune with the other New Testament writings.

Translations

The Old Testament was written in the Hebrew language (most of it, some small parts in Aramaic). There came a time when many Jews could not speak Hebrew because of the Greek influence in their society, so a translation of the Hebrew Old Testament was made in the Greek language. It was called the "Septuagint" (seventy) because it was produced by 70 scholars.

During New Testament times the people spoke in Aramaic which was an ancient language of Palestine. The books and letters of the New Testament were not written in this language however, they were written in the common form of Greek (Koine), which was the universal language of the period.

The Greek form of the New Testament remained the standard as copies were made from the original and distributed for the first several centuries. There are 5357 complete and partial Greek manuscripts in existence today. These are the documents that scholars who produce translations into various languages work with at the present time.

With time, the Greek was translated into Latin and other languages, but these translations were always made from the original Greek manuscripts.

Latin was the language of the western portion of the Roman Empire and as Christianity spread westward from its original home (where Greek was the dominant language) a new version of the Bible was developed (the Greek Orthodox Church still uses the Septuagint version of the Old Testament).

In 404 AD a new Latin version of the Bible was produced by Jerome, an early church leader. His translation from Greek to Latin was called the Latin Vulgate. This term was used because Jerome used common rather than formal Latin for his translation. This became the standard version for study and church life in the Middle Ages.

Various translations were made into common languages from the 5th to 14th centuries. These included Gothic, Syrian, Slavic, English, French, German, Italian and Spanish translations.

In the 14th century the Renaissance movement sparked a renewed interest in the Greco-Roman world's languages and literature. This produced a greater effort to examine Greek culture and resulted in a revival of the knowledge of Greek and Hebrew languages as well as a study of the ancient biblical manuscripts. One important result of this renewed interest in ancient languages was a zeal to produce new Bible versions in common languages translated directly from the original Greek and Hebrew. All of this activity was helped along by a powerful religious movement called the Reformation.

With the invention of the printing press in 1436, the technology to actually produce mass quantities of Bibles in different languages was realized.

It is interesting to note that the very first book to be printed on Gutenberg's new invention was the Latin Vulgate version of the Bible sometime between 1452 and 1455. This Bible was called the 42-line Bible because there were exactly 42 lines on each page. It still exists today and can be seen at the Gutenberg Museum in Frankfurt, Germany.

The invention of the printing press helped spread the Bible in various languages throughout the world.

The earliest known English translation was produced in 700 AD. (A Latin version with English notes between the lines.) The first English translation was done by John Wycliffe in 1382, he was imprisoned for his efforts. The first printed English Bible was William Tyndale's in 1526. There were many translations as the science of translation and archeology developed. A major translation of the time was the King James Bible in 1611. It became the authorized version for English speaking people for many years, and is still one of the most popular Bibles today.

Many other translations have appeared over the years and each has a different style:

- **Revised Standard Version**: A good Old Testament, but the New Testament is a little awkward.

- **American Standard Version**: Best word-per-word translation, but the English is complicated.

- **New American Standard Version**: Easy to read while retaining accurate translation from the original languages.

- **New International Version**: English flows well, but some find it too general.

- **New Living Translation**: Paraphrases rather than translates.

There are many other translations aside from these as each generation tries to more accurately translate the Word of God for easy understanding.

Some say you cannot trust any translation because translators are human and can make mistakes. Of the thousands of translations in different languages, there are no major doctrines, persons or commands that are in conflict or question. If there are mistakes, they are punctuation, names of places or locations, etc., which are obscure in the original languages as well.

The percentage of error in today's translations from the Greek text is less than $1/10$ of 1%. When we are reading the English or French versions for example, we are reading 99 $9/10$ % of what is written in the Greek and Hebrew. We can trust the particular translation of the Bible we are reading because it accurately tells us what God is saying.

Summary

We have reviewed:

- How the early church decided which books belonged in the New Testament canon.

- What events motivated them to do this.

- What criteria they used to select the material.

- The division of the New Testament.

- Some information on how the Greek and Hebrew were translated into modern languages.

In our next chapter we will look at the content of the Bible and answer the question, "Why do we believe that it is inspired?"

CHAPTER 3
SIX PROOFS OF INSPIRATION

So far we have covered several areas related to the history of the making of the Bible. These include:

1. The history of writing itself. This topic is important because it proves the existence of writing in Old Testament times.

2. The history of book making. The three significant advances in this area that included the codex form, the printing press and the internet.

3. How the Old Testament was formed. This history is significant because it is what Jesus and the Apostles used to state their case concerning the Messiah and His coming (Acts 18:28).

4. Finally, how the New Testament books were collected and organized, and what criteria was

used to determine which books would be included in the accepted canon. We also looked at the translation of the New Testament into various languages over the centuries and how these were made.

By the year 367 AD the entire Bible, as it now is organized, was accepted as the authoritative Word of God. No additions or changes have been made since then, and whether people agree or not on the contents, there is no disagreement (except for Muslims, Mormons and Jehovah's Witnesses who say the Bible was corrupted, and that they have a new revelation) that the 66 books contained in this volume make up the Bible and has done so for about 1600 years.

Our last question is this, "Why do we believe that this book is inspired by God?" We believe and can show that it is an old book and a book recorded by certain people, but how do we know that it is a book given to us by God Himself? There are six different "proofs" that indicate that this book is inspired.

PROOF #1
The Bible Claims to be Inspired

The Old Testament takes this idea of divine inspiration for granted since it continually describes dialogue between God and man. The New Testament, however, states the idea in different ways:

> [19] But when they hand you over, do not worry about how or what you are to say; for it will be given you in that hour what you are to say. [20] For it is not you who speak, but it is the Spirit of your Father who speaks in you.
> - Matthew 10:19-20

Jesus told His Apostles that the content of what they would say would come from God. This counters the idea that the Bible is simply the product of human thought.

> But the Helper, the Holy Spirit, whom the Father will send in My name, He will teach you all things, and bring to your remembrance all that I said to you.
> - John 14:26

This passage speaks to the "how" the Apostles spoke from God: they were directed by the Holy Spirit. The Apostles recorded the teachings and actions of Jesus over a three-year period without error or contradiction; this was done with the help of the Holy Spirit.

Inspiration is a miraculous thing and John records that the Holy Spirit is the One that made this miracle happen, like He did for other miracles.

> All Scripture is inspired by God and profitable for teaching, for reproof, for correction, for training in righteousness;
> - II Timothy 3:16

Paul, the Apostle, says that all of scripture is inspired. Some try to eliminate the creation account in Genesis or the accounts of miracles because of modern scientific skepticism, but the Bible says that it is fully inspired, not partially so.

> 20 But know this first of all, that no prophecy of Scripture is a matter of one's own interpretation,
> 21 for no prophecy was ever made by an act of human will, but men moved by the Holy Spirit

spoke from God.
- II Peter 1:20-21

The Bible says of itself that its writing was never man's idea or written by his impulses or intelligence. God chose which men to write and selected what they would write.

The Bible says that it is not only a book about religion written by pious men, but the very communication between God and man. A person can choose not to believe that the Bible is inspired, but no one can deny that this is what the Bible says about itself.

Inspiration Theories

When considering the idea of inspiration, the question is often asked, "How did God inspire people to write the Bible?" There are several theories about exactly how God moved men to write the scriptures.

Dictation Theory

This theory says that God dictated, word for word, everything that is in the Bible. Man was unconscious of God's knowledge and simply wrote down the words exactly as they were given to him by God.

The problem with this idea is that there are different styles and qualities of writing among the various authors. For example, Isaiah is more poetic than Mark, and Luke's Greek is more polished than Peter's. If God dictated the Bible word per word, it would seem that each book would be equal in its composition, style and language.

Thought Theory

This theory proposes that God provided the general ideas and principles, and the writers interpreted these in their own words. This theory says that it is the thought or the general concept that is important and if some things seem contradictory or difficult, the mistakes belong to the human writers.

Of course if we admit errors in the details (years, locations, events, etc.), how can we have confidence in the general concepts? God does not do things halfway. He does not make mistakes in general principles or in details. An inspired work is perfect from beginning to end in general as well as in specific details. It is hard to trust a work that acknowledges mistakes.

Verbal Inspiration

This theory says that God revealed the true knowledge to the patriarchs, prophets, Apostles and other Bible writers, and they wrote this information down under the guidance of the Holy Spirit. The reason that each book has a different style and polish is the same reason that a particular song may have a different style and polish depending on what instrument it is played upon, a harp or a kazoo. The reason that pictures of the same object look different usually depends on the materials you use to reproduce it (oils, watercolors, crayons, pencil, photograph, poem, etc.).

This is why Peter, the rough fisherman from Galilee, writes a simple straightforward account of what happened to Jesus through his secretary Mark. This is why Luke or Paul, the educated men, weave intricate, detailed histories of their lives and teaching in a dozen letters.

> [11] For who among men knows the thoughts of a man except the spirit of the man which is in him? Even so the thoughts of God no one knows except the Spirit of God. [12] Now we have received, not the spirit of the world, but the Spirit who is from God, so that we may know the things freely given to us by God, [13] which things we also speak, not in words taught by human wisdom, but in those taught by the Spirit, combining spiritual thoughts with spiritual words.
> - I Corinthians 2:11-13

In this passage Paul is talking about the inspiration process experienced by those who were used by God to record His word.

The Holy Spirit guarded the Apostles and others from error, but allowed them to write in their own language, in their own style, and with their own conscious personalities. However, the mind, the ideas, the concepts, the commands, the details and the theology came from God.

When we say the Bible is inspired, here is what is meant:

1. The purpose, ideas, knowledge, direction, commands, teachings and visions all come from God.

2. The decision as to who would write what, when and where it was written came from God.

3. The ability to remember, to describe accurately, to include all information necessary was given by God to men through the Holy Spirit in a miraculous way.

4. The men who actually recorded the Bible wrote according to the language, education and style that they possessed as human beings in the era and place where they lived.

Summary of Proof #1

The Bible says that it is from God, but the fact that it claims this is not proof that it does. However, it is a first step that points us in that direction. The fact that the Bible itself says that it is an inspired book establishes the criteria by which we are to judge it.

The next set of proofs support this basic contention to a point where a person can look at the evidence and conclude that the Bible is indeed from God and not merely a human production.

PROOF #2
History of the Bible

A strong indicator that the Bible is not an ordinary book, that it is indeed supernatural in character, is its ability to survive violent attack and close scrutiny without being destroyed or discredited.

Attack by the Roman Empire

From 249-305 AD it was a capital offence to be in possession of any portion of Scripture. This is why copies from this period were small and easy to hide. By the 4th century Constantine, Emperor of Rome, permitted and paid for copies to be made. The Bible survived the most powerful empire in history that was bent on destroying it and, yet, survived, even prospered.

Attack by the Roman Catholic Church in Middle Ages

The Roman Catholic Church tried to keep people from reading or possessing the Bible because they felt it was too dangerous. In many cases, Bibles were chained to pulpits so no one would steal them. By the 16th century King James paid for a translation and distribution of the Bible in a common language and broke the monopoly of the Roman Catholic Church. The Bible survived the repression of the most powerful religious organization in the Middle Ages.

Attack by the Philosophers, Skeptics and Critics

In the 17th to 19th centuries writers and thinkers in Europe began to question the Bible's inspiration and authority. They developed godless ideas about where man originated and how he should live. One of these, Voltaire, a brilliant French philosopher said, "It took 12 ignorant fishermen to establish Christianity and one Frenchman to destroy it." His personal crusade was to discredit the Bible as uninspired and draw people away from using it as their guide for life. Twenty-five years after his death, his home was purchased by the Geneva Bible Society and used as a warehouse to distribute Bibles.

If we look at the history of the Bible we see that it has survived military, religious and philosophical attacks over a 2000 year period and continues to be the most printed, most translated, most read book in the world and in all of history. Of course, you would expect this from a book that says of itself that it is from God.

PROOF #3
Uniqueness of the Bible

Whenever scholars examine "religious" books they always discover flaws, mistakes, the inability of the teachings to apply to all people or adapt to changing times.

One reason why many religions like Shinto or Zoroastrianism die out is that their teachings become irrelevant or unworkable in changing times. Muslims protect themselves against this because they say that the Koran was actually written by God in a special language and no non-Muslim can touch it or understand it properly. However, many scholars agree that the Muslim religion has many inconsistencies and without changes cannot survive or be adapted to western countries.

The Bible, however, has been translated, examined and re-examined by scholars and experts in each century. These all come to similar conclusions about the uniqueness of the Bible. For example:

1. **The Bible is unique in its depths of insight and beauty.** Dr. George White from Harvard University said that in comparison with other holy books in modern and ancient times, the Bible is in a class by itself. There is no comparable book or class of writings. It is deep enough for the most learned scholar and simple enough for a child to grasp.

2. **The Bible is unique in its unity.** 66 books, 1400 years to write, 40 authors writing at different times and places, most not knowing each other, yet the entire book tells only one story without contradiction, confusion or

disorder. It is as if only one person wrote it, and, of course, only one person did, God.

3. **The Bible is unique in its universality.** The Bible is the most read, most translated, most sold book in the history of the world without exception. There are still over 5000 partial and complete copies of original biblical manuscripts that exist. No other ancient book has this many in circulation that are this old. It has had universal appeal for over 1900 years.

No other book can claim as many readers in as many centuries in as many languages for as many years. No other book has been so studied and found to be so unique in style, content and unity. You would expect this from a book written by God.

PROOF #4
It Works

This is a modern man's criteria; something is true or good because it works. With this in mind, one cannot deny the fact that the principles contained in the Bible do work to produce happy and peaceful lives. No other philosophy, lifestyle or religion works better. All you have to do is examine non-Christian countries to see this.

For example, the United States prospered when it was functioning under Christian principles found in the Bible and has begun to falter as the nation has moved away from these. You would expect that God's manual for life would lead to a superior life for a person or a nation that follows it. Simply compare any person or nation not following the Bible and it will be plain to see that God's plan for life is in the Bible and nowhere else.

PROOF #5
Historical Exactitude

If a book is inspired it has to be accurate because God does not make mistakes. Archaeology supports the historical accuracy of the Bible. Archaeology is the study of people, customs and life in ancient times. They do this by digging up and studying the remains of ancient cities, villages, temples, etc.

Whenever archaeologists discover a city or people mentioned in the Bible, everything they find out in their discovery is in harmony with what the Bible describes about these people. Actually, archaeologists use the Bible as a reference guide to search out many of these ancient places.

For example, Joshua 3:10 mentions the Hittites, but until recent history archeologists had not found any trace of this civilization. This was one of the arguments used to reject the historical accuracy of the Bible. In 1872 however, archeologists discovered Hittite writings and the remains of their cities which confirmed their existence and Bible accuracy concerning these people.

Sometimes historians find out that their discoveries do not contradict the Bible, they simply do not have all the pieces of the puzzle. For example, Isaiah 20:1 mentions Sargon. His name was not in any of the historical records of the Kings of that time, but recent discoveries have shown that he borrowed his name and this fact was only recorded in the Bible, and not the records kept by historians of that era.

The key idea of this historical evidence is that if the Bible has been shown to be accurate in obscure historical facts, is it not logical to trust its accuracy in other matters as well? Men have tried to undermine its accuracy for centuries and have always failed. You would expect that kind of razor sharp accuracy from a book written by God, would you not?

PROOF #6
Fulfilled Prophecy

Men cannot accurately predict future events. They can study trends and make predictions based on these hoping to have a percentage of success. Only God, however, can be 100% successful in predicting future events. In the Bible there are many predictions or prophecies of events in the lives of people and nations that would take place days, years and centuries into the future. For example, here is one of Isaiah's prophecies:

> "It is I who says of Cyrus, 'He is My shepherd!
> And he will perform all My desire.'
> And he declares of Jerusalem, 'She will be built,'
> And of the temple, 'Your foundation will be laid.'"
> -Isaiah 44:28

Isaiah lived in 700 BC. The Cyrus that he speaks of is a king that will rule 150 years later. He names him, gives his position and explains what he would eventually do (allow the captive Jews to return to their land and rebuild the temple in Jerusalem). This would be like me predicting what the name and party of a president would be a century in advance.

There are hundreds of such prophecies in the Old Testament and of these 61 deal specifically with Jesus; His racial lineage (Jeremiah 23:5), time when He would come (Daniel 2:31-45), the place He would be born (Micah 5:2), titles and power (Isaiah 9:6-7), His character, ministry and death (Isaiah 42-52).

How is fulfilled prophecy evidence that the Bible is from God?

1. Accurate fulfillment of a prophecy is a sign that a supernatural power is at work. Some have guessed at the future, but no man has produced hundreds of accurately detailed and fulfilled prophecies. Only God can do this, and He has done so in the Bible.

2. The Bible is the only holy book that contains a record of fulfilled prophecy. No other religion has this feature. There are many holy books and writings by pious men and women, but only the Bible has a record of both prophecies made and their fulfillment hundreds of years later, all confirmed by history (Isaiah did live and write in the 7th century, Cyrus did live and reign and kept the Jews captive in the 6th century).

If the Bible is from God, would you not expect that it contains a feature that only God could produce? A feature like fulfilled prophecy?

Summary

Let us review briefly the arguments that point to the divine inspiration of the Bible:

1. It says of itself that it is inspired by God.

2. It has survived 2000 years of criticism, scrutiny and attack; something no other book has done.

3. It has been found to be unique among all writings in every area, psychologically, emotionally, theologically, historically, socially, etc.

4. It has changed the lives of individuals and nations.

5. It is exact in all its details.

6. It contains fulfilled prophecy, a phenomenon not duplicated by mere man.

What conclusion do we come to in the face of such evidence? That mere man or a group of people wrote this book? If so, why have men never been able to duplicate, improve or destroy this book? We have improved, duplicated or destroyed everything else, except the Bible. The only conclusion is to believe what is says, that it is truly a book from God and the evidence is sufficient to support this.

If, after considering these things, we accept that the Bible is inspired, then there are several things required of us:

1. We must not simply study or read the Bible, but rather understand that it is God who speaks to us and we can know Him through the Bible.

2. We must not simply hear the Bible, but rather put it into practice because it is God Himself who is calling us to be baptized, to live pure lives, to love our neighbor and be ready for His return.

3. We must not be afraid. The world may not believe and may try to destroy the Word of God, but it is the rock upon which our faith is built and no storm can overcome those who stand upon it (Matthew 7:21).

Conclusion

The first and foremost Christian doctrine is the inspiration of the Bible. If this is not true, then the teaching that comes from the Bible has no power or final authority. This is why there are so many attacks against it.

In the next chapter we will look at the second great Christian doctrine: the divinity of Christ.

MAJOR CHRISTIAN DOCTRINES

I. Inspiration of the Bible
II. Divinity of Christ

CHAPTER 4
WHAT THE BIBLE SAYS ABOUT JESUS

In this chapter we will examine the second great Christian doctrine: the divinity of Jesus Christ. There are many theories about Jesus and who He was: a Jewish Rabbi, a prophet of some kind, a ghost or spirit, even an alien or some kind of advanced life form. Christians, however, believe that the Bible teaches that He is the divine Son of God.

The Bible's Central Theme

The inspired Bible is about Jesus Christ. He is the main theme and character spoken of in the Scriptures. He is the main point of all the books of the Bible. The different parts of the Bible serve to explain different things about Him and His interaction with us.

1. The Old Testament is really the story of the creation of the world, the creation and fall of mankind, and how God prepared for the coming of Jesus by the formation of the Jewish nation. All the events in the Old Testament set a human and historical stage for His eventual appearance as a man in this world. The Scriptures tell this story through the eyes and words of Jewish prophets, leaders and kings.

2. The four gospels are the eyewitness accounts of His life, ministry, death, resurrection and ascension back to heaven. Again, the story is recorded and preserved by men who were with Jesus for years and who knew Him intimately.

3. The rest of the New Testament, written by other apostles and disciples, shows how His followers established the Christian church according to Jesus' instructions. In addition to these, there are teachings to help followers/disciples live the Christian life in every generation and cultural setting.

We could go anywhere in the Bible to find out about Jesus concerning:

- The promise of His coming.

- The preparations for His appearance.

- The circumstances of His miraculous birth.

- The content of His teachings.

- The details of His death and resurrection.

- The people who knew Him personally and spread His teachings throughout the world.

I do not think, however, that we would have the time in a single chapter to do this. What we can do is focus on what the Bible says about who Jesus is. This is the first step in establishing His divinity. This is actually the most important question about Jesus Christ, and we will see what three individuals written about in the Bible say about Jesus.

Who is Jesus?

Now remember, we are asking the question, "Who is Jesus?" according to the Bible and not just based on what we think, feel, learned from a book, movie or teacher concerning His person. Since most of the direct and eyewitness accounts about Him are in the New Testament portion of the Bible, let us go there to learn about Him.

Thousands of people saw and heard Jesus speak, teach and even do miracles. There is no doubt of His existence because historians of that era write about Him and His ministry. For example, Josephus Flavius, a Jewish historian who wrote about this period, mentions Jesus' death by crucifixion and the activities of His disciples at that time. He was not a follower of Jesus but includes Him in his writings.

History (not from the Bible) writes that Jesus was a Jewish man born into a humble family who lived in Israel approximately 2000 years ago. He began His ministry by claiming that He was the Jewish Messiah/Savior and was eventually arrested and executed by the Roman government at the insistence of the Jewish leaders who accused Him of causing civil unrest. Eventually His followers established the Christian church based on His teachings. This is what history books tell us about the facts of His life.

There were others, however, who actually followed Jesus as His special disciples and they too recorded their accounts of His life. It is from these writers, whose records form the New Testament, that we can establish a much more comprehensive picture of who Jesus really was.

For the sake of our study we will examine three of these men's writings concerning Jesus.

Witness of the Apostles

Peter

The first of these is Peter. Peter was a fisherman by trade, and along with his brother, Andrew, had a family business. He was the first "Apostle" called by Jesus to follow Him on a full time basis.

He would eventually hear all of Jesus' teachings, witness His miracles and, later on, be a leader in establishing the church. He died as a martyr in Rome claiming to the very end that what he heard and saw was true.

During His ministry Jesus asked His Apostles who they thought He was? Peter answered without hesitation, "You are the Messiah, the Son of the Living God" (Matthew 16:16). While Jesus was alive, the Bible says that Peter believed and declared Him to be the divine Son of God.

Later on, after Jesus was executed, Peter described the things that he saw with his own eyes as he rebuked the Jews for their hard hearts and disbelief.

[14] But you disowned the Holy and Righteous One and asked for a murderer to be granted to you, [15] but put to death the Prince of life, the one whom God raised from the dead, a fact to which we are witnesses.

- Acts 3:14-15

There is much written about Peter in the New Testament, and Peter himself writes two of the books/epistles contained in this part of the Bible. But the two passages just mentioned summarize well what Peter thought about Jesus based on what he experienced:

1. That Jesus was the Christ/Messiah/Savior promised in the Old Testament. In other words, Jesus was the one sent by God to save mankind.

2. Peter also concluded that Jesus was divine based on what he heard Jesus say and what he saw Him do.

3. Finally, Peter saw Jesus executed by Roman soldiers and then saw Him after God raised Him from the dead.

Peter never changed or denied this witness, even when he was threatened, imprisoned and finally sent to his death for saying these things.

When we want to know who Jesus is, the Bible, through Peter's words, says that He is the Son of God, the Savior, the One resurrected from the dead.

Thomas

Another Apostle we know less about was Thomas. He is the one often referred to as "doubting Thomas" because he wanted proof of Jesus' resurrection before he would believe. What he says about Jesus is interesting because of this very fact; he demanded proof before he would continue to believe.

He knew Jesus and, like the other Apostles, had lived and worked with Him for three years. He saw the miracles, heard the teachings and witnessed Jesus die on the cross. He was convinced Jesus was dead, so brutal and final was His execution at the hands of the Roman soldiers.

When the other Apostles reported that they had seen Jesus resurrected and alive again, Thomas was skeptical and refused to believe. In the gospel of John, we read about Jesus' confrontation with Thomas and how Thomas was encouraged to believe.

[24] But Thomas, one of the twelve, called Didymus, was not with them when Jesus came. [25] So the other disciples were saying to him, "We have seen the Lord!" But he said to them, "Unless I see in His hands the imprint of the nails, and put my finger into the place of the nails, and put my hand into His side, I will not believe."

[26] After eight days His disciples were again inside, and Thomas with them. Jesus came, the doors having been shut, and stood in their midst and said, "Peace be with you." [27] Then He said to Thomas, "Reach here with your finger, and see My hands; and reach here your hand and put it into My side; and do not be unbelieving, but believing." [28] Thomas answered and said to Him,

"My Lord and my God!"
- John 20:24-28

Note what this exchange teaches us about Jesus:

1. Thomas believed that Jesus had actually risen from the dead.

2. Thomas acknowledged that Jesus was God, not just a prophet, teacher or holy man.

3. The Apostles demonstrated that Jesus was worthy of not only belief, but worship as well.

4. Thomas, in calling Jesus Lord, indicated that Jesus had authority over him.

Once again, a short passage, but one where the Bible sets forth the important facts about who Jesus is: divine, object of belief and worship, Lord over us.

People are free to choose whether they believe this or not, but the fact remains that this is what the Bible teaches about Jesus.

Paul

Perhaps no one, other than Jesus Himself, articulates in more detail the character and person of Jesus Christ than Paul the Apostle.

Paul was a Jew and an early persecutor of the Christian church. As a Pharisee he was part of the ruling class in the Jewish society of Jesus' day. He was a religious zealot for Judaism who had obtained a mandate from the ruling council of Jewish leaders to wage a campaign of persecution against Christians in order to discourage the spread of this faith.

In recounting his own experience, Paul describes the meeting with Jesus Christ that changed his life:

[1]"Brethren and fathers, hear my defense which I now offer to you."

[2] And when they heard that he was addressing them in the Hebrew dialect, they became even more quiet; and he said,

[3] "I am a Jew, born in Tarsus of Cilicia, but brought up in this city, educated under Gamaliel, strictly according to the law of our fathers, being zealous for God just as you all are today. [4] I persecuted this Way to the death, binding and putting both men and women into prisons, [5] as also the high priest and all the Council of the elders can testify. From them I also received letters to the brethren, and started off for Damascus in order to bring even those who were there to Jerusalem as prisoners to be punished.

[6] "But it happened that as I was on my way, approaching Damascus about noontime, a very bright light suddenly flashed from heaven all around me, [7] and I fell to the ground and heard a voice saying to me, 'Saul, Saul, why are you persecuting Me?' [8] And I answered, 'Who are You, Lord?' And He said to me, 'I am Jesus the Nazarene, whom you are persecuting.' [9] And those who were with me saw the light, to be sure, but did not understand the voice of the One who was speaking to me. [10] And I said, 'What shall I do, Lord?' And the Lord said to me, 'Get up and go on into Damascus, and there you will be told of

all that has been appointed for you to do.' [11] But since I could not see because of the brightness of that light, I was led by the hand by those who were with me and came into Damascus.

[12] "A certain Ananias, a man who was devout by the standard of the Law, and well spoken of by all the Jews who lived there, [13] came to me, and standing near said to me, 'Brother Saul, receive your sight!' And at that very time I looked up at him. [14] And he said, 'The God of our fathers has appointed you to know His will and to see the Righteous One and to hear an utterance from His mouth. [15] For you will be a witness for Him to all men of what you have seen and heard. [16] Now why do you delay? Get up and be baptized, and wash away your sins, calling on His name.'
-Acts 22:1-16

And thus began the conversion and mission of one of the most prolific of Jesus' Apostles. We know, both from history and from the Bible, that Paul went on to preach and establish the Christian religion throughout the Roman Empire. He was eventually imprisoned by the Emperor Nero and executed in Rome in 67 AD on account of his role as a Christian leader. Paul, the adversary of the church, the one who initially denied who Jesus was, ended up giving his life for his faith in Christ.

In his writings we have a very dynamic description of Jesus and His exalted position:

[15] He is the image of the invisible God, the firstborn of all creation. [16] For by Him all things were created, both in the heavens and on earth, visible and invisible, whether thrones or

dominions or rulers or authorities—all things have been created through Him and for Him. [17] He is before all things, and in Him all things hold together. [18] He is also head of the body, the church; and He is the beginning, the firstborn from the dead, so that He Himself will come to have first place in everything.
- Colossians 1:15-18

Note what Paul specifically says about who Jesus is:

1. **Visible image of God.** When you see Jesus you are looking at God.

2. **Existed before creation.** He exists before time, like God; eternal.

3. **Supreme over creation.** He has the authority of God.

4. **He is the agent of creation.** Everything in the material and spiritual world was created by and for Him.

5. **He is the head of the church.** Jesus is the only leader of the church in heaven and on earth. He does not share this with any other person.

6. **He leads those who will resurrect.** This was another way of saying that Jesus is eternal. In declaring that He leads in the future, Paul says that He is already there.

These things are not the only things Paul says about Jesus, but we can see from these that Paul was proclaiming Jesus as the divine Son of God based on his own experiences and knowledge of Christ and His teachings.

The Testimony of Jesus

Aside from these three witnesses concerning the person of Jesus Christ we have one other individual's testimony to examine and that is the witness of Jesus Himself. Our description would not be complete without examining what Jesus said about His true identity.

Here are three things that Jesus said about Himself to three separate individuals.

The Samaritan Woman

In a conversation with the woman at the well, Jesus answers a question about the identity of the true Messiah.

> [25] The woman said to Him, "I know that Messiah is coming (He who is called Christ); when that One comes, He will declare all things to us." [26] Jesus said to her, "I who speak to you am He."
> - John 4:25-26

Jesus describes Himself as the Savior spoken of by the Jews.

Peter

We have looked at Peter's declaration earlier in this chapter, but this time let us focus on Jesus' response to what Peter says.

> [15] He said to them, "But who do you say that I

am?" [16] Simon Peter answered, "You are the Christ, the Son of the living God." [17] And Jesus said to him, "Blessed are you, Simon Barjona, because flesh and blood did not reveal this to you, but My Father who is in heaven.
- Matthew 16:15-17

Note that Jesus confirms what Peter says about Him and even goes on to reveal how Peter has come to this realization.

The Apostles

After His resurrection and appearance to over 500 disciples, Jesus gives His Apostles (and future disciples) their mission.

[18] And Jesus came up and spoke to them, saying, "All authority has been given to Me in heaven and on earth. [19] Go therefore and make disciples of all the nations, baptizing them in the name of the Father and the Son and the Holy Spirit, [20] teaching them to observe all that I commanded you; and lo, I am with you always, even to the end of the age."
- Matthew 28:18-20

Note that in this passage Jesus claims exclusive authority over all.

These are only a few of the teachings that are recorded concerning Jesus, but from these we see some of the things the Bible says about Him. Aside from being a true historical figure, Jesus is also:

- The Jewish Messiah

- The Son of God

- The Lord God Himself (divine)

- Resurrected from the dead

- An eternal being

- The agent of creation

- The head of the church

- The supreme authority in heaven and earth

I could add more information concerning Jesus contained in the Bible, but I will close this chapter with a quote from the gospel of John who faced a similar dilemma (trying to list all the things he actually heard and saw Jesus do). Faced with the mountain of information before him, John writes in the 20th and 21st chapters of his gospel record:

> [30] Therefore many other signs Jesus also performed in the presence of the disciples, which are not written in this book; [31] but these have been written so that you may believe that Jesus is the Christ, the Son of God; and that believing you may have life in His name.
> - John 20:30-31
>
> And there are also many other things which Jesus did, which if they were written in detail, I suppose that even the world itself would not contain the books that would be written.
> - John 21:25

CHAPTER 5
THE RESURRECTION
AS PROOF

In the previous chapter we began to look at the second great Christian doctrine in our series: the divinity of Jesus Christ. We examined the internal (biblical) evidence concerning this claim and saw that very much like the first great Christian doctrine (biblical inspiration), the second great Christian doctrine (divinity of Christ), finds its first proof within the Bible itself. In other words, the Bible claims that Jesus was divine and we examined several key persons who made this claim:

- The prophets who spoke of His divinity when they prophesied concerning the coming Messiah (Psalm 110:1; Psalms 16:8-11).

- The Apostles who witnessed His miracles, resurrection and ascension, and recorded their experience.

- And then, of course, there is Jesus in dialogue with others who claims this about Himself, and does so when facing the Jewish leaders who were trying to trap Him in order to find an excuse to execute Him.

> [63] But Jesus kept silent. And the high priest said to Him, "I adjure You by the living God, that You tell us whether You are the Christ, the Son of God." [64] Jesus said to him, "You have said it yourself; nevertheless I tell you, hereafter you will see the Son of Man sitting at the right hand of Power, and coming on the clouds of heaven."
> - Matthew 26:63-64

I again repeat what I said about the Bible's claim of inspiration: A person is free to reject the notion that Jesus Christ is divine, that He is God, but cannot deny that this is what the Bible says about Him. If you asked the question, "What does the Bible say about itself?" The answer would be, "The Bible says that it is the inspired Word of God." In the same way if you asked, "What does the Bible say about Jesus?", it would say that He is, among other things, the divine Son of God. Again, just saying so does not make it so, but the Bible offers one unmistakable proof: His resurrection from the dead!

The Resurrection - Proof of Divinity

In the gospels the writers describe many of Jesus' teachings and miracles that support the claim that He was from God and doing God's will. However, many other prophets and servants of God did miracles, spoke from God, even raised people from the dead (Elijah, I Kings 17:23).

But the sign and proof that God provided to confirm Jesus as divine was His resurrection from the dead.

> [1] Paul, a bond-servant of Christ Jesus, called as an apostle, set apart for the gospel of God, [2] which He promised beforehand through His prophets in the holy Scriptures, [3] concerning His Son, who was born of a descendant of David according to the flesh, [4] who was declared the Son of God with power by the resurrection from the dead, according to the Spirit of holiness, Jesus Christ our Lord,
> - Romans 1:1-4

Even Jesus Himself gave this as the ultimate sign pointing to His true identity.

> [38] Then some of the scribes and Pharisees said to Him, "Teacher, we want to see a sign from You." [39] But He answered and said to them, "An evil and adulterous generation craves for a sign; and yet no sign will be given to it but the sign of Jonah the prophet; [40] for just as Jonah was three days and three nights in the belly of the sea monster, so will the Son of Man be three days and three nights in the heart of the earth.
> - Matthew 12:38-40

In discussing Jesus' identity, we need to look at His resurrection and the many ways that God used this miracle. We often say that Jesus had to die in order to free us from sin. In the same way, He had to resurrect in order to provide several proofs or evidences.

Why Jesus had to Resurrect

He had to resurrect to prove who He was.

If I ask someone, "Who is Jesus Christ?" The answer would be, "Jesus is the Son of God" or, "He is divine" or, "He is the Messiah." Now, if I were to ask, "What proof do you have that He is divine, or that He is the Messiah, the Son of God?" What would you answer then?

If you said that your proof was His wonderful teachings, His many miracles, His kindness and goodness, your answers would be incomplete. Jesus did all these things, but the Bible does not present these as the final proofs of His divinity or the signs that He was the Messiah. No, the Bible says that His resurrection from the dead was the undeniable event that God established as the one true sign of His divine nature.

Paul explained this to the philosophers and thinkers in Athens when he preached to them saying:

> because He has fixed a day in which He will judge the world in righteousness through a Man whom He has appointed, having furnished proof to all men by raising Him from the dead.
> - Acts 17:31

Paul told them that the proof that God provided all men that Jesus was the legitimate savior and judge was His resurrection. Yes, the miracles, the teachings, the life, all pointed to His true identity, but Jesus' resurrection was the primary evidence given by God.

This was not something new, the fact that resurrection from the dead was to be the key sign pointing to the true Messiah and Savior was also spoken of by the prophets long before Jesus' arrival. Isaiah spoke of the necessary suffering, death and resurrection of the Messiah (Isaiah 53). Peter quotes David's Psalm 16:8-11, where David prophesizes concerning the eventual resurrection of God's righteous one.

Paul summarizes this entire argument in the first few verses of his letter to the Romans:

> [1] Paul, a bond-servant of Christ Jesus, called as an apostle, set apart for the gospel of God, [2] which He promised beforehand through His prophets in the holy Scriptures, [3] concerning His Son, who was born of a descendant of David according to the flesh, [4] who was declared the Son of God with power by the resurrection from the dead, according to the Spirit of holiness, Jesus Christ our Lord,
> - Romans 1:1-4

Many prophets and special servants of God spoke the words of God, lived good lives, performed mighty miracles and even raised people from the dead. Many have begun religious movements with millions of followers. Many have died as martyrs defending their causes or their gods. But only Jesus Christ actually rose from the dead according to prophecies made about Him. No one ever prophesied about Mohammad's coming or the Buddha, but the prophets spoke of Jesus and His resurrection.

Jesus had to resurrect in order to prove that He was indeed the one true divine Messiah sent by God to save all men, spoken of by the prophets.

When someone questions your faith in Jesus and why you believe that He, and only He, is the divine Son of God, your answer should be that you believe because God has provided His resurrection as proof of His true identity.

He had to resurrect to demonstrate His sinlessness.

Paul the Apostle summarized what the relationship between sin and death was. He said:

> For the wages of sin is death, but the free gift of God is eternal life in Christ Jesus our Lord.
> - Romans 6:23

In other words, the result or outcome of sin is the eventual decay and death of the body, and the separation of the soul from God. It does not matter if one knows this law or not, it is in operation. This is much like the law of gravity. Whether one knows the scientific details of gravity or not, ignorance of the principles of gravity does not save a person in the event that they fall over a cliff. In the same way, ignorance or denial of God's law of sin and death does not save one from the consequences of this law.

Jesus was executed, and when the Roman officials were sure that He was dead (they put a spear into Him and blood and water poured out signifying death), they placed Him in a tomb. Had Jesus gone straight to heaven from the tomb, many could have accused Him of not being without sin since death had the last say in His life (the law of sin and death took effect). When I die and am put into the ground, there will be no doubt that I was a sinner. My death is proof that I had a sinful flesh for a certain number of years.

Had Jesus remained in the tomb, the same conclusion would have been drawn about Him.

Now, someone may ask, "What is so important about Jesus being without sin?" That Jesus was without sin was important because in order to make a sacrifice good enough to remove all of our sins, that sacrifice, that life offered, had to be perfect and without a single sin. Paul says it this way:

> For as through the one man's disobedience the many were made sinners, even so through the obedience of the One the many will be made righteous.
> - Romans 5:19

Paul is referring to Adam and Jesus here; he says that Adam forfeited his life by disobedience (which is sin), and that all of his descendants became subject to death. Eventually, Jesus was sent by God, and by His obedience (meaning He was without sin), He was able to recover the life that Adam lost as well as the lives of those subject to death because of Adam's disobedience.

When Peter gets up on Pentecost Sunday to preach the gospel, he begins his sermon by establishing the fact that Jesus rose from the dead because death could not hold him.

> But God raised Him up again, putting an end to the agony of death, since it was impossible for Him to be held in its power.
> - Acts 2:24

Before going on to offer the good news of forgiveness and reconciliation, Peter demonstrates that Jesus, through His sacrifice and resurrection, could legitimately offer this gift.

Jesus had to rise from the dead to prove that His was indeed a perfect and sinless sacrifice able to remove the sins from our imperfect lives. (We will talk more about this system of atonement in another chapter.)

Without His resurrection we could not be sure that what He did actually could accomplish what He said it would.

He had to resurrect to prove that we could resurrect.

I love makeover shows on TV. Take someone and re-do their hair, make-up, their clothes and a remarkable change takes place. This type of program is especially effective when they are trying to sell exercise videos or diet books. Have you noticed what they do? They show a video or picture of someone who is 200 pounds overweight and then bring them out after their weight loss. They talk about the special diet, exercise book or DVD that helped get that result. And you buy the stuff. Why? Because you believe. Why? Because you saw the transformation before your very eyes, that is why!

Imagine if they showed this 500 pound guy on a video and then claimed he was down to 195 pounds of pure muscle, but you had no picture, no credible witness, just the company's word for it. The commercial would sound something like this: "Tony would love to be here to show you how buff he is, but he is at the beach today!" Would you buy the stuff now? Maybe, but if you did not have a picture, it would be quite a stretch would it not?

From the moment Adam and Eve were removed from the perfect harmony of the Garden of Eden, man's greatest fear has been the fear of death. He fears it because it is associated with suffering and the unknown.

People try to deal with death in many ways. They go into denial by living exclusively to enjoy their existence here on this earth; they try to be philosophical and accept death's inevitability. But no one has managed to come back from the dead. Not just an incident where they were clinically dead for a few moments while their hearts stopped, I mean dead and buried for a few days and then come back to say what death was like.

Well, no one except Jesus Christ, that is. And the good news He brings is that we do not have to be afraid of death anymore because it is not final, there is life after the experience of death, and His resurrection is proof.

The Hebrew writer explains it this way:

> [14] Therefore, since the children share in flesh and blood, He Himself likewise also partook of the same, that through death He might render powerless him who had the power of death, that is, the devil, [15] and might free those who through fear of death were subject to slavery all their lives.
> - Hebrews 2:14-15

Because we feared death, Satan seduced us into all kinds of behavior that set our hope and love on this world and this life only. However, through His resurrection Jesus showed that death had been conquered and we could be free to look forward to another life and a better place than this life and this place.

77

Jesus' resurrection showed everyone that resurrection from the dead was indeed possible. Jesus went one step further than merely proving that He had the power to resurrect, He also offered resurrection to everyone who desired it.

> For this is the will of My Father, that everyone who beholds the Son and believes in Him will have eternal life, and I Myself will raise him up on the last day.
> - John 6:40

Jesus could have gone straight to heaven to be with the Father and sent out the Apostles to preach resurrection for all believers, but without a demonstration it would have been very difficult to believe. Jesus had to resurrect to show us, who are hard of heart and slow to believe, that our resurrection would indeed be possible because of His.

Summary

The second great Christian doctrine is the divinity of Jesus Christ:

1. The Bible claims it.

2. The resurrection proves it.

3. The eyewitness accounts of the Apostles and disciples record it.

4. The fact that neither the Jews nor the Romans could find the missing body, and that even under threat of torture and death the original eye witnesses refused to recant, confirms it.

Every attempt to destroy the Christian religion begins by attacking the two foundational doctrines of the Christian faith: the inspiration of the Bible and the divinity of Christ. This is why it is important to know them because if we do, we can then confidently review and accept as true the other great Bible doctrines.

MAJOR CHRISTIAN DOCTRINES

I. Inspiration of the Bible
II. Divinity of Christ
III. Original Goodness
IV. Fall of Man
V. Reconciliation

Chapter 6: The History of Mankind in Three Doctrines

CHAPTER 6
THE HISTORY OF MANKIND IN THREE DOCTRINES

We have reviewed the first two great biblical doctrines of inspiration of the Bible and the divinity of Christ. The other great Bible doctrines are based on these.

In this chapter we begin to study the next three great Bible doctrines together because they form a set:

- The Doctrine of Original Goodness

- The Doctrine of the Fall of Man

- The Doctrine of the Restoration or Reconciliation of Man to God

These three doctrines could be summarized as follows: In the beginning God created the universe and man to be good. Man disobeyed God and consequently was separated from God and made subject to suffering and death, along with all creation. Since then, God has acted in human history in a dynamic way in order to reconcile man to Himself through Jesus Christ.

Original Goodness

The first of this set of three is the doctrine of original goodness, and it is found in Genesis chapters one and two.

> [26] Then God said, "Let Us make man in Our image, according to Our likeness; and let them rule over the fish of the sea and over the birds of the sky and over the cattle and over all the earth, and over every creeping thing that creeps on the earth." [27] God created man in His own image, in the image of God He created him; male and female He created them.
> - Genesis 1:26-27

Man is created in the likeness of God. This explains his potential and ability for doing what is good, creative, etc. It also explains why the most evil of people have some good. For example, Hitler was a painter, and terrorists love their families. Man's basic character begins as good.

> God blessed them; and God said to them, "Be fruitful and multiply, and fill the earth, and subdue it; and rule over the fish of the sea and over the birds of the sky and over every living thing that moves on the earth."
> - Genesis 1:28

Man is God's partner in the management of creation and he is good at it. So man's purpose and work are good.

> [16] The Lord God commanded the man, saying, "From any tree of the garden you may eat freely; [17] but from the tree of the knowledge of good and evil you shall not eat, for in the day that you eat from it you will surely die."
> - Genesis 2:16-17

Man is given a moral code in order to define his limits. This moral code gives substance to his relationship with God. Man has free will but was not free to disobey God; this is the limit of his freedom. The ethical code given to man awakened the conscience part of his being and provided the perspective as to the difference between himself and God.

We have heard of the saying, "I think therefore I am" (René Descartes). Well, the reason I think is because God gave me the ability to choose. The ability to choose provides the moral tension that enables man to experience self-awareness and a primary experience of God.

> Then the Lord God said, "It is not good for the man to be alone; I will make him a helper suitable for him."
> - Genesis 2:18

A perfectly suitable partner was given to man in order to share in the joy of life and management of creation. Mankind's life and enjoyment was good.

The biblical view of man is that he was designed as a holy, godly being and his task was to choose (as a conscious act of his will) to remain good, holy and obedient to God. Without this ability he is like the animals, aware only of himself, but not of God.

This, then, is the third major doctrine of the Bible: the doctrine of original goodness of man.

- He was created to have a relationship with God.

- He was created with the ability to manage creation and produce a society.

- He was created with the capacity to choose good and avoid evil.

- He did not just know God's will, he had the ability to do it if he chose to.

The Fall of Man Through Sin

The fourth major doctrine of the Bible, and second in our subset of three, is man's fall from grace through sin.

The original position of Adam and Eve at creation saw them having an intimate relationship with God as well as a perfect natural, emotional and spiritual balance between themselves, the creation and their creator. This prefect balance was destroyed when they fell through their disobedience to God.

When the woman saw that the tree was good for food, and that it was a delight to the eyes, and that the tree was desirable to make one wise, she took from its fruit and ate; and she gave also to her husband with her, and he ate.
- Genesis 3:16

Through deception and seduction woman and man are tempted to disobey God, and they do. God's command establishes what is right and wrong, violating His will constitutes sin and always has negative consequences. This, in essence, is the substance of the fourth great biblical doctrine. Man has been given the ability to choose and choosing to obey will result in maintaining his position. Choosing to disobey will result in a fall, and this fall is the subject of this doctrine.

> [7] Then the eyes of both of them were opened, and they knew that they were naked; and they sewed fig leaves together and made themselves loin coverings. [8] They heard the sound of the Lord God walking in the garden in the cool of the day, and the man and his wife hid themselves from the presence of the Lord God among the trees of the garden. [9] Then the Lord God called to the man, and said to him, "Where are you?" [10] He said, "I heard the sound of You in the garden, and I was afraid because I was naked; so I hid myself." [11] And He said, "Who told you that you were naked? Have you eaten from the tree of which I commanded you not to eat?" [12] The man said, "The woman whom You gave to be with me, she gave me from the tree, and I ate." [13] Then the Lord God said to the woman, "What is this you have done?" And the woman said, "The serpent deceived me, and I ate."
> - Genesis 3:7-13

Note how this passage describes the results of their fall:

- Rebellion (disobedience)
- Shame (hiding)
- Anger (this woman you gave me)

- Loss of innocence and love (defensive attitude)
- In addition to these, note the unbalancing of the social, natural and emotional order that existed between God and man, man and woman, and man and creation. This disruption ultimately resulting in physical and spiritual death.

The doctrine of the fall of man through sin is mirrored throughout the entire Old Testament: Cain and Abel, the sinfulness leading to the flood, the cycle of destruction that follows the Jewish nation throughout history; all reflect the fall of man through sin.

Misinterpretation of Major Doctrine

The fourth major doctrine has been misunderstood and improperly taught to the point that entire doctrinal systems have evolved around the incorrect application of its core ideas. One teaching that misrepresents the doctrine of the fall of man is the doctrine of "Original Sin."

Original sin

This doctrine was originally formulated by Augustine, a 4th century theologian, who mixed Christian doctrine with Greek philosophical ideas. He taught that Adam's fall produced two things:

1. **A human nature which was unable by itself to choose good or to respond to God in faith.** This idea, later developed by Protestant thinkers (Calvin/Presbyterianism) as "total depravity" said that without the direct intervention of the Holy Spirit a person was not able to obey God.

2. The second idea Augustine promoted was that **original sinfulness and its condition of moral helplessness was passed on (or imputed) to every descendant of Adam.** In other words, every child born afterwards was not only born guilty of Adam's sin, but helpless to do anything about it.

After a time, several practices grew out of this false thinking:

Infant baptism and baptism for the dead

Those who accepted this idea of original sin reasoned that if people were born guilty, they were then condemned at birth and needed to be saved immediately. They also reasoned that if you could impute (pass on) guilt, you could also impute faith. The idea was that if Adam's sin transferred to you, it seemed reasonable that your parent's faith could be transferred to you as well in order to save you.

From here it was easy to conclude that if you, as a baby, could be saved without being conscious of it, you could also be saved after you die (i.e. baptism for the dead).

Another false idea that grew out of this incorrect interpretation of the doctrine of the fall of man is that of predestination/arbitrary election.

Predestination / Arbitrary Election

The doctrine of total depravity created a problem. If one was unable to respond to the gospel because sinners were too depraved to do so, how could one be saved? In answer to this question Augustine, and later some of the Protestant Reformers, taught that God chose, in advance, those who would be lost and those who would be saved. The rationale was that since you were helpless to choose or obey, the only way to be saved was if God arbitrarily chose you for salvation.

Now another question that arises at this point is, "If God chooses me, how do I know that I have been chosen?" Evangelicals (Baptists, Community Churches, etc.) see God's choice of themselves for salvation by observing the progressive improvement of their moral character as a confirmation that one has been chosen. This is why there is a "watch and see" period before baptism, and why they teach that baptism is not essential for salvation (you have already been chosen, baptism is only a symbolic ritual).

The idea of "once saved, always saved" comes from the teachings on original sin. After all, if God chooses you, you cannot refuse (irresistible grace) and you can never fall (once saved, always saved).

Charismatic and Pentecostal churches see the ability to speak in tongues as the sign of election by God. It is the way they know and are sure of God's choosing of them.

The teaching of the incorrect idea of original sin was a departure from the biblical doctrine of the fall of man. It said that by his fall, Adam spread the guilt for sin to all men. It said that because of this guilt, man became unable to choose correctly (depraved) or to respond to God in faith. It taught that God arbitrarily chose some for salvation and others for condemnation; and once the choice was made, nothing could change it.

Eventually this led to modern religious groups looking for signs of improved moral living or special spiritual gifts as an assurance that they were the chosen. This is why Evangelicals say, "I accept Jesus as my Savior."

They accept because they cannot choose. Roman Catholics respond to this doctrine by baptizing babies. Since babies cannot save themselves, the parents save them based on their transferred faith.

We will examine these departures again later, but for now let us go back to our discussion of this set of major doctrines.

The first two doctrines in this set of three teach us about man's original goodness when created, and the consequences of his fall through the sin of disobedience.

The second doctrine (fall through sin) has been used to establish a variety of other doctrines such as original sin, total depravity and election, as well as certain religious practices like infant baptism.

However, in its original form, the doctrine of the fall of man simply explained that from the beginning man had the power to choose right from wrong, and even after the fall, continued to have this ability, even if it was weakened by a sinful nature. This is where we, in the Churches of Christ, differ from most Protestants and Evangelicals.

The Bible clearly teaches the idea that each is responsible for their own sins:

> But your iniquities have made a separation
> between you and your God,
> And your sins have hidden His face from you so
> that He does not hear.
> - Isaiah 59:2

It is the individual's sins that condemn him, not those of others.

> [20] The person who sins will die. The son will not bear the punishment for the father's iniquity, nor will the father bear the punishment for the son's iniquity; the righteousness of the righteous will be upon himself, and the wickedness of the wicked will be upon himself.
>
> [21] "But if the wicked man turns from all his sins which he has committed and observes all My statutes and practices justice and righteousness, he shall surely live; he shall not die.
> - Ezekiel 18:20-21

The gospel appeals to man's intellect and requires a choice based on faith. Something only an adult can do. Baptism is a ritual that expresses obedient faith.

> [3] This is good and acceptable in the sight of God our Savior, [4] who desires all men to be saved and to come to the knowledge of the truth.
> - I Timothy 2:3-4

God requires that all men be saved, not just a few, not just those chosen for this.

Man still has the capacity to accept or reject Christ. His spiritual destiny is in his hands where God originally placed it at the creation. Christ died for all men and all those who believe in Him, repent of their sins and are baptized will be saved (Matthew 28:18-20, Acts 2:37-38). Man's spiritual destiny is in his own hands.

Summary

If we could read the Bible in one sitting, we would note how naturally and seamlessly these three great doctrines follow each other. The first two describe and explain man's original goodness followed by his sin, his fall and the consequences of these. The third major doctrine in the set explains the wonderful story of how God restores man to Himself (restoration of sinful man).

> [17] Therefore if anyone is in Christ, he is a new creature; the old things passed away; behold, new things have come. [18] Now all these things are from God, who reconciled us to Himself through Christ and gave us the ministry of reconciliation, [19] namely, that God was in Christ reconciling the world to Himself, not counting their trespasses against them, and He has committed to us the word of reconciliation.
> - II Corinthians 5:17-19

The word reconciliation means to bring into harmony or to re-align. The history and the method that God used in reconciling man with Himself after the fall is what the rest of the Bible is about and the subject of the fifth major doctrine (and the third in this set of three).

This reconciliation between God and man is explained in the ten sub-doctrines of:

A. Election (biblical)

B. Predestination (biblical)

C. Atonement

D. Redemption

E. Regeneration

F. Adoption

G. Justification

H. Perfection

I. Sanctification

J. Salvation

The next several chapters of this book will be a study of the sub-doctrines that explain God's plan and purpose in reconciling fallen mankind to Himself.

We will look back at what these mean, why God did it this way and how these impact our Christian lives.

MAJOR CHRISTIAN DOCTRINES

I. Inspiration of the Bible
II. Divinity of Christ
III. Original Goodness
IV. Fall of Man
V. Reconciliation
    A. Election
    B. Predestination

Chapter 7: Error and Consequence

CHAPTER 7
ERROR AND CONSEQUENCE

Let us quickly review what we have done so far. The last three major doctrines that we have examined, which are a set, are:

1. **Original Goodness:** Man is created good and he is responsible and able to remain as such (he has the ability to choose).

2. **The Fall Through Sin:** Man becomes subject to suffering, death and condemnation because of disobedience, but retains the ability to choose right from wrong and the ability to respond to God.

3. **Reconciliation to God Through Jesus Christ:** God works throughout history to save man. This process of reconciliation is explained in ten sub-doctrines which are the subject of our continuing study.

In this chapter we will discuss the first two sub-doctrines, Election and Predestination.

Election

The word election simply means, "to choose" (like in politics). Biblical election in the process of reconciliation refers to the choice that God made from the beginning in connection with the reconciliation of man to Himself. Election is about God's choice, not ours.

The choice (or election) that God made is based on His character and will. His character is dominated by love (I John 4:7-8). The love in His character requires that His creation be reconciled to Him.

> [4] who desires all men to be saved and to come to the knowledge of the truth. [5] For there is one God, and one mediator also between God and men, the man Christ Jesus,
> - I Timothy 2:4-5

God's election/choice, motivated by His love, is that all men be saved and thus reconciled into a relationship with Him.

In order to fulfill His will, God made a choice, not that some would be saved and some lost. He chose or elected Jesus Christ to be the One through whom everyone could be saved.

The doctrine of election centers on Christ, not on us. Jesus is the only "elected" one. The doctrine of election does not explain how God saves us, just who He chose to accomplish this task.

> [4] And coming to Him as to a living stone which has been rejected by men, but is choice and precious in the sight of God, [5] you also, as living stones, are being built up as a spiritual house for a holy priesthood, to offer up spiritual sacrifices acceptable to God through Jesus Christ. [6] For this is contained in Scripture:
>
> "Behold, I lay in Zion a choice stone, a precious corner stone, And he who believes in Him will not be disappointed."
> - I Peter 2:4-6

The Greek word "*elektos*" means selected, elected or chosen. Some translations have this word translated into English as "precious," but this does not convey its meaning. In context it means that something was previously selected, not simply valuable.

God chose/elected/selected Jesus as the instrument through whom His creation would be saved. Every other choice made by God (i.e. Noah, Abraham, prophets, servants like Samson, etc.) was made in order to serve His purpose of bringing Jesus Christ, His chosen/elected one, to earth in order to reconcile mankind to Himself.

The Jewish nation was a stage upon which God would put His Chosen One in order to accomplish this task. These people were not selected to be saved or lost. They were called to serve God's purpose and had the ability to respond or reject God's offer to participate in the plan to bring God's Son to earth. For example, Saul, Israel's first king, was chosen by God to serve in this capacity but disobeyed God and was ultimately replaced by David, another chosen servant who did obey. One other example of this process was Judas, the Apostle and traitor, who did not believe and rejected his opportunity to serve God in proclaiming Christ.

For centuries much of Protestant and subsequent Evangelical doctrine has had at its base the concept that "election" meant that God arbitrarily chose some for salvation and others for damnation; and once the choice was made no one or no thing could undo that choice.

John Calvin, an early Protestant leader and writer, wrote in his Institutes of Christian Religion III.21, "...it is now sufficiently plain that God, by His secret counsel, chose whom He will save while He rejects others."

The Savoy Declaration of 1658, III.3 of the English Catechism puts forth the same idea, "...by the decree of God for the manifestation of His glory, some men and angels are predestined to everlasting life, and others preordained to everlasting death."

One reason for these conclusions concerning election was that this idea was interpreted in light of Augustine's teaching concerning original sin (all men are born guilty of sin and without the ability to choose right or obey the gospel, so God is required to choose/elect those who will be saved and those who will be lost).

Now that we understand some of the mistakes made in interpreting biblical election, let us look at what the Bible says about this idea.

God has chosen Christ through whom He desires to save all men

> [4] who desires all men to be saved and to come to the knowledge of the truth. [5] For there is one God, and one mediator also between God and men, the

100

man Christ Jesus,
- I Timothy 2:4-5

And coming to Him as to a living stone which has
been rejected by men, but is choice and precious
in the sight of God,
- I Peter 2:4

When God chooses or elects, He chooses or elects
Christ to come and save mankind. Christ is the only
choice that God makes.

⁵ Therefore, when He comes into the world, He
says,
"Sacrifice and offering You have not desired, But
a body You have prepared for Me;
⁶ In whole burnt offerings and sacrifices for sin
You have taken no pleasure.
⁷ "Then I said, 'Behold, I have come
(In the scroll of the book it is written of Me)
To do Your will, O God.'"
- Hebrews 10:5-7

God offers all men the opportunity to be saved through Jesus Christ

¹⁸ And Jesus came up and spoke to them, saying,
"All authority has been given to Me in heaven and
on earth. ¹⁹ Go therefore and make disciples of all
the nations, baptizing them in the name of the
Father and the Son and the Holy Spirit,
- Matthew 28:18-19

He who has believed and has been baptized shall be saved; but he who has disbelieved shall be condemned.
- Mark 16:16

God wants all to be saved, and He offers everyone this opportunity. Every person who is of the age of reason and of a right mind has the ability to respond. The gospel is not beyond our understanding or ability to obey. We are asked to give an ascent of our own will in believing, and we can do this.

Those who are united to Christ by faith share in His election

26 For you are all sons of God through faith in Christ Jesus. 27 For all of you who were baptized into Christ have clothed yourselves with Christ.
- Galatians 3:26-27

3 Blessed be the God and Father of our Lord Jesus Christ, who has blessed us with every spiritual blessing in the heavenly places in Christ, 4 just as He chose us in Him before the foundation of the world, that we would be holy and blameless before Him.
- Ephesians 1:3-4

I am back to my example about politics. We choose one candidate to run for office. Those who vote for him share in his victory if he/she wins. God chose Christ. He wins the victory over sin and death, and we share in His victory, not because God chose us, we share in victory because we chose Christ through faith expressed in our obedience to the gospel. We become the elect, the chosen ones because of our union with Christ, the only chosen one of God. This union or association with Christ is accomplished through faith in Him as the Son of God. This faith is expressed when we confess our faith in Jesus, repent of our sins, and are baptized in His name (Acts 2:38).

This elect status we receive by virtue of our union with the elected One is not something God does arbitrarily. We become the elect/the chosen ones because we choose to respond to the gospel, which results in our unity with the elected One.

The Restoration Movement (digression)

This teaching about the freedom to choose, the ability to respond to the gospel, and the potential of salvation for all men is what fired up the early Restoration Movement in the 18th and 19th centuries, and from which our present fellowship of the Churches of Christ comes.

Alexander and Thomas Campbell, Barton W. Stone along with John Smith were preachers and Presbyterian ministers in Europe and in early America. Their study of the Scriptures moved them away from the Calvinistic point of view and led them to preach that God loved all men and wanted all to be saved. They taught that through simple faith and obedience to the gospel (which was possible for everyone) any person could be saved.

If you read their histories, you will find that they were censured and put out of their Presbyterian churches. Because of this they left their roots and began forming their own congregations calling themselves Christians and began to do away with other religious traditions that had no basis in the Bible.

By the middle of the 20th century the Churches of Christ that grew out of this Restoration Movement were the fastest growing religious group in America within what was referred to as Christianity. The reasons for its success was the belief that God wanted all men saved, the belief that all had the ability to respond to the gospel, and the effort by the church to share the gospel with all.

In recent years, the church has slowed its growth because it has moved away from this principle. When we begin to doubt the universality of sin and the need for all to be saved, we lose our edge for evangelism and church growth is impeded.

Predestination

Closely linked to the doctrine of election is that of predestination. Again, before I explain the biblical concept of predestination I need to review with you what was understood as predestination as it was erroneously taught in connection with the doctrine of "Original Sin."

Calvinists taught that predestination meant that God knew, in advance, who He would choose for salvation and who He would choose for damnation. In order to get a clearer picture, let us first look more carefully at the meaning of the word itself. Predestination is the foreknowledge of a final result. For example, I exercise foreknowledge in the fact that if I put my hand in the fire, it will burn. I know this result before the event.

Predestination as a doctrine in the process of reconciliation refers to God's knowledge of the final result or the end of a matter. More specifically, it means that He knows the final result that His choice will produce.

> For those whom He foreknew, He also predestined to become conformed to the image of His Son, so that He would be the firstborn among many brethren;
> - Romans 8:29

> He predestined us to adoption as sons through Jesus Christ to Himself, according to the kind intention of His will,
> - Ephesians 1:5

God knew that His choice of Christ as the One to accomplish salvation would result in the salvation of all those united to Him. He foreknew that sin would lead to death. He predestined that all who believed in Christ would be saved.

In still other words, predestination expresses the idea that God knew from the very beginning that His choice of Jesus would have the result of reconciling mankind to Himself.

A practical example of predestination at work:

1. I want to satisfy my desire for ice cream. (My will expresses itself.)

2. I choose a Dairy Queen banana split to be the way my will is to be satisfied. I choose a way to satisfy my will. (I elect/choose.)

3. I predestine/foreknow that the result of my choice will satisfy my will. (I will enjoy the Dairy Queen, it will satisfy my desire.)

This is how God's election and predestination work; His will is satisfied by His choice. It works perfectly for Him because He is perfect. It does not always work this way for us for many reasons. For example, human will is not always reliable: we do not know what we want, or if what we want is good for us (for example, ice cream is too fattening, there may be no bananas that day or the Dairy Queen is closed for repairs). I have no way of knowing these things so my foreknowledge is limited.

God, however, has exercised His will in perfect accord with His justice and mercy. What He wants for us is perfect, loving and gracious. God's choice/election is also perfect. He chooses Christ who cannot fail in accomplishing God's will and fulfilling His foreknowledge.

Our faith is based on the sureness of God's election and predestination. If He chooses Christ to save us, Christ will succeed in that task. If His knowledge says that all who are united to Christ by faith expressed in repentance and baptism will be saved, then those who believe in Jesus and are baptized will be saved.

God knows for sure that His plan to reconcile us through Christ will work. He does not force us to choose, He does not make the choice for us. We do the choosing to believe and obey, or not. Our spiritual destiny is in our own hands. God merely knows the results because He is eternal and guarantees us eternal life with Him if we choose Christ, the one He has chosen and guaranteed to save us.

Summary

- **Election** - This is a Christ centered doctrine, not man centered. God chooses Christ, not men. The only people He chooses are chosen to serve His plan, not chosen for salvation. Some chose to serve, others refused, but the choice to serve was theirs.

- **Predestination** - This refers to a divine characteristic of God wherein He knows in advance the end result of choices He has made, as well as the choices we have made. He knows the results, but he does not force us to choose.

These are comforting teachings because they assure us that the choices God calls on us to make are based on His limitless and loving foreknowledge.

MAJOR CHRISTIAN DOCTRINES

I. Inspiration of the Bible
II. Divinity of Christ
III. Original Goodness
IV. Fall of Man
V. Reconciliation
    A. Election
    B. Predestination
    C. Atonement

Chapter 8: God's Method of Reconciliation

CHAPTER 8
GOD'S METHOD OF RECONCILIATION

The fifth biblical doctrine, reconciliation, says that God is restoring man to Himself through Jesus Christ. The following sub-doctrines explain the process of this reconciliation.

The sub-doctrine of Election explains how God chose Jesus Christ as the instrument through whom He would offer salvation to all men.

The sub-doctrine of Predestination describes the fact that God knew in advance that those who would be united to Christ by faith would be reconciled to Him.

In other words, when we put these two doctrines together we could say, "God always knew that those in Christ would be saved."

I also mentioned that the value of the Restoration Movement is that this is where these biblical doctrines were rediscovered and taught to the masses.

In this chapter we will study the sub-doctrine of atonement. This sub-doctrine explains the method that God used to accomplish reconciliation.

The word atonement comes from a Greek word which means to reconcile or to cause a change or an exchange. It is a change on the part of one party induced by the action on the part of another.

In the Bible the doctrine of atonement refers to the death of Jesus Christ as the means by which God and man became one and were restored to a state of friendly relationship. God changed His attitude towards man because of what Jesus did. God chose Jesus to accomplish atonement.

Here is how atonement works:

The Problem

[1] Behold, the Lord's hand is not so short
That it cannot save;
Nor is His ear so dull
That it cannot hear.
[2] But your iniquities have made a separation
between you and your God,
And your sins have hidden His face from you so
that He does not hear.
- Isaiah 59:1-2

Sin produces estrangement between God and man, like a wall that separates a couple if there is the sin of adultery. Man has betrayed God through sin.

The Extent

Sin is a universal phenomenon.

> for all have sinned and fall short of the glory of God,
> - Romans 3:23

> [12] Therefore, just as through one man sin entered into the world, and death through sin, and so death spread to all men, because all sinned— [13] for until the Law sin was in the world, but sin is not imputed when there is no law. [14] Nevertheless death reigned from Adam until Moses, even over those who had not sinned in the likeness of the offense of Adam, who is a type of Him who was to come.
> - Romans 5:12-14

The Result

The end result of sin is estrangement. It is a comprehensive separation that includes man and nature (environment disrupted), mankind itself (wars), as well as man and God (guilt, fear). The final result of this estrangement is death (separation of the soul from the body, and separation of the soul from God).

> For the wages of sin is death, but the free gift of God is eternal life in Christ Jesus our Lord.
> - Romans 6:23

The Solution

Reconciliation with God.

> For while we were still helpless, at the right time
> Christ died for the ungodly.
> - Romans 5:6

There needs to be reconciliation with God in order to avoid spiritual death and permit some reconciliation between all of the other elements of the creation.

The death on the cross by Jesus is the action that brought about the change in God's relationship with sinful man. In other words, what Jesus did changed what God felt or how He viewed man.

Key question: Why not just forgive or destroy everybody? God is sovereign, who would dare question Him?

Answer: The problem with either of these solutions is found in God's character. He is perfect and perfectly balanced.

His perfect sense and execution of justice require that His laws be obeyed and the natural consequences of disobeying His laws be allowed to happen. His core law, revealed in the garden, said that disobedience leads to separation from Him (death).

> [16] The Lord God commanded the man, saying,
> "From any tree of the garden you may eat freely;
> [17] but from the tree of the knowledge of good and
> evil you shall not eat, for in the day that you eat
> from it you will surely die."
> - Genesis 2:16-17

This is a core law and if God simply changed the law or suspended its consequences, He would not be perfect in justice. The fact that no one obeys perfectly is not a reason to change or suspend the law.

Another part of God's character is His perfect love. It was love that moved God to create the world, and it was this same love that moved Him to save the world He lovingly created.

> For God so loved the world, that He gave His only begotten Son, that whoever believes in Him shall not perish, but have eternal life.
> - John 3:16

The problem here can be stated in the following way: how can God express His perfect love in reconciling sinful man to Himself without violating His perfect sense of justice which demands satisfaction for breaking the law of God?

A further complication is that even with the knowledge of his disobedience and willingness to be reconciled to God, man is unable to make up for his disobedience and remove his own guilt and condemnation.

God cannot violate the terms of His justice and let man go free, so what is needed is a solution that will satisfy, at the same time, both justice and mercy.

And so, the doctrine of atonement is the teaching that explains how God resolved this dilemma.

The Method = Atonement

> and He Himself bore our sins in His body on the

cross, so that we might die to sin and live to righteousness; for by His wounds you were healed.
- I Peter 2:24

In this short verse Peter summarizes the doctrine of atonement. Jesus offers Himself up as a sinless sacrifice to pay the moral debt of all men. Let us break this idea down.

For the wages of sin is death, but the free gift of God is eternal life in Christ Jesus our Lord.
- Romans 6:23

Jesus' sacrifice satisfies God's perfect justice because the payment for all sin is made. The law that requires a price to be paid for disobedience has been satisfied once for all time. Disobedience causes death, and a death has been offered.

[9] By this the love of God was manifested in us, that God has sent His only begotten Son into the world so that we might live through Him. [10] In this is love, not that we loved God, but that He loved us and sent His Son to be the propitiation for our sins.
- I John 4:9-10

God's perfect love is also satisfied in that He offers His own Son as sacrifice in order to rescue us from condemnation and death. In the cross of Christ, we see the perfect balance of God's justice and mercy working harmoniously in order to bring about reconciliation. The death of Jesus on the cross, this is the action which satisfies God's justice/debt for sin and changes His attitude from one of condemnation to one of forgiveness towards sinners. Unless the debt/justice is satisfied, there can be no forgiveness, and Jesus pays that debt. He makes atonement.

Personal Atonement

Many people think that they are fairly good, moral, decent people and are consequently right with God. We need to realize that no matter how good or moral we are, we could never atone for our own sins with our own lives, even if that life had many good and sincere deeds.

God's justice requires a sinless life to be offered, not just a pretty good life. The reason for this goes back to Adam. He was sinless when he was created and through sin he forfeited that sinless life. Everyone born after Adam is less than he was because the sin that began with him has spread to us. A sinless life needs to be offered up for the perfect life that was given to and forfeited by him. This is only just. One sinless life offered for one sinless life lost due to sin.

> [12] Therefore, just as through one man sin entered into the world, and death through sin, and so death spread to all men, because all sinned
>
> [18] So then as through one transgression there resulted condemnation to all men, even so through one act of righteousness there resulted justification of life to all men.
> - Romans 5:12, 18

No one, therefore, could live a perfect life and have such a life to offer as atonement, no matter how nice and moral they were. Even if a person wanted to offer their life, it would not be good enough to satisfy God's demand of a perfect life. This is why Jesus had to come in order to first, live a human life without sin, and then offer it to God through death as a payment for the life Adam forfeited through sin.

In addition to the perfection of His life, Jesus was also divine in nature so the value of His life was without measure (i.e. it is an issue of purchasing power: one pound of gold has greater purchasing power than one pound of copper). The perfect nature of Jesus' life made His sacrifice acceptable. The divine nature of His life made His sacrifice valuable to the extent that it atoned not only for Adam's sin, but for every sin committed for all time by all men.

There have been many people who have lived good lives and have even sacrificed their lives to save the lives of others, but only Jesus has both a perfect and divine life to offer God in exchange for the souls of all men.

The Language of Atonement

There are a variety of ways to express the action and results of the doctrine of atonement. For example, payment for the debt of sin equals atonement; satisfaction of God's justice equals atonement; sacrifice of Jesus on our behalf equals atonement.

There are many other expressions that explain the idea that Jesus' sacrifice on the cross satisfies God's justice and permits Him to express His love towards us by offering forgiveness and reconciliation. The atonement of Christ demonstrates that we could never satisfy God's justice and obtain forgiveness on our own, Jesus does this. We can, however, accept the forgiveness offered to us by God, now that Jesus has made restitution on our behalf.

> and He Himself bore our sins in His body on the cross, so that we might die to sin and live to righteousness; for by His wounds you were healed.
> - I Peter 2:24

It is important to understand that Jesus has made full restitution for all of our sins. We cannot add or contribute to His payment for sin in any way with good deeds, sincerity or personal sacrifice.

Many people are under the impression that repentance is our way to make restitution to God. They believe that we make restitution through our repentance, and whatever we cannot do, Jesus makes up for it on the cross. Salvation is not a twelve-step program for alcoholics where they try to go back and make things right with people they have harmed with their addiction. This may help mend relationships with people here on earth, but does not repair the separation from God on account of these failures.

The doctrine of atonement teaches that Jesus' sacrifice makes restitution to God for all of our sins.

> Now why do you delay? Get up and be baptized, and wash away your sins, calling on His name.
> - Acts 22:16

Note here that Saul, the persecutor of Christians is told to wash away all his sins. Why? Jesus made restitution to God for all the evil Saul had done. We have no record of Saul going back to apologize or make restitution to anyone.

Atonement is how God deals with the restitution due to Him for all of our sins, especially those that are sometimes impossible to fix, like adultery, abortion, etc. Jesus' restitution is the only way to have peace when guilty of unfixable sins.

This is what we mean when we say that we cannot contribute anything towards our salvation, towards paying the price or making restitution to God. Like the song says, "Jesus paid it all." Atonement is the doctrine that this song is talking about.

So someone will say, "What about repentance, what about baptism?" Of course these have a place in the process of reconciliation, but we do not exchange these for our sins. In other words, repentance and baptism are not acts that make restitution for our sins. The cross of Christ does this.

Reconciliation is possible because restitution has been made by Jesus on our behalf and is offered on the condition that God has always required from His people, faith.

Reconciliation and forgiveness are offered to us based on our faith, not our personal goodness, or sacrifice or our ability to make restitution for our sins. God offers reconciliation to us based on faith because Christ has made restitution for us with His atoning death on the cross. We have only faith to offer because we cannot give anything else. The consent of our wills is all we have.

This faith is expressed in the following way:

1. Belief

We are asked to believe who Jesus is and what God has done for us through Him.

> For God so loved the world, that He gave His only begotten Son, that whoever believes in Him shall not perish, but have eternal life.
> - John 3:16

2. Repentance

Repentance is a conscious decision to do away with sin in our lives, to acknowledge it because of Christ.

> Peter said to them, "Repent, and each of you be baptized in the name of Jesus Christ for the forgiveness of your sins; and you will receive the gift of the Holy Spirit.
> - Acts 2:38

3. Confession

Our belief leads us to acknowledge Jesus as the Lord and the Christ. We do not confess our sins; God knows our sins; we confess our faith in Christ.

> 36 As they went along the road they came to some water; and the eunuch said, "Look! Water! What prevents me from being baptized?" 37 [And Philip said, "If you believe with all your heart, you may." And he answered and said, "I believe that Jesus Christ is the Son of God."]
> - Acts 8:36-37

4. Baptism

Baptism is an immersion in water in the name of, or because of our faith in Christ. Baptism cleanses the conscience because it is done by faith in Jesus.

> He who has believed and has been baptized shall be saved; but he who has disbelieved shall be condemned.
> - Mark 16:16

5. Faithfulness

Christians are called to remain faithful to Christ until death.

> You will be hated by all because of My name, but it is the one who has endured to the end who will be saved.
> - Matthew 10:22

Faith is the active ingredient that gives these expressions their power. Responding to God with a proper expression of faith is not a "work" or "legalism," it is faith obeying in love.

There are many ways to express one's faith in God. Religions in the world have created thousands of different actions, traditions, ceremonies, etc. that are expressions of faith in a supreme being.

However, the five things I have mentioned are the ways that Jesus has taught that men are to respond to Him. Faith in Him and faith to receive forgiveness require these expressions; all others are useless since they are not given by Jesus.

Summary

Man is helpless because he is a sinner and will ultimately be condemned by God for it. Even if he wanted to, he could not give to God the perfect life necessary to pay for his sins, let alone the divine life to pay for everyone's sins.

God solves this problem by sending Jesus to live a perfect life and offer it up in death as a payment for the sins of men (this is what the doctrine of atonement explains).

Because of this, God is now free to offer forgiveness to all men through Jesus Christ.

This faith is properly and effectively expressed through belief, repentance, confession, baptism and faithfulness.

When we combine the first three sub-doctrines of election, predestination and atonement in one sentence, we can say: "God always knew that those in Christ would be saved by His atonement."

MAJOR CHRISTIAN DOCTRINES

I. Inspiration of the Bible
II. Divinity of Christ
III. Original Goodness
IV. Fall of Man
V. Reconciliation
    A. Election
    B. Predestination
    C. Atonement
    D. Redemption

Chapter 9: What Atonement Achieves

CHAPTER 9
WHAT ATONEMENT ACHIEVES

This book about Christian doctrines is like a puzzle where each chapter adds an additional piece in order to complete the picture.

So far, these are the pieces that we have in place:

1. We are studying the major doctrines into which all the stories and teachings of the Bible can be fitted.

2. We began with the doctrine of the inspiration of the Bible and the doctrine of the divinity of Christ. Next we studied:

   - The doctrine of original goodness: God creates the world and man as good.

- The doctrine of the fall: Man willfully disobeys God and sets into motion the deterioration of himself and of the creation.

- The doctrine of reconciliation: God works throughout history in order to save and reconcile man back to Himself.

The bulk of our study has focused on this fifth major doctrine that has ten sub-doctrines which explain why, how and for what purpose God has reconciled man to Himself. We have looked at three of the sub-doctrines under reconciliation:

A. Election: The doctrine that teaches us that God chose or elected Christ to be the One through whom He would save and reconcile mankind.

B. Predestination: The doctrine that teaches that God knew in advance that His plan to reconcile man would work.

C. Atonement: The doctrine that explains that the "method" God would use to achieve reconciliation would be the death of one in exchange for the life of another.

In this chapter we will study the fourth sub-doctrine, the doctrine of redemption.

Redemption: Word Meaning

A simple way to define the idea of redemption is to say that it is what Christ achieves with His atonement. Atonement is the act and redemption is the result.

The word in the Greek translated into the English word redemption means, "to be freed, liberated, ransomed, acquitted or released." The basic ideas represented by this word are:

- To buy back something that has been forfeited because one has failed to pay a debt. (For example, the bank seizes your car because you have not made the payments. You redeem your car and get it back by paying up all the back debts, interest and penalties.)

- To liberate or set free those either ruled by a higher authority or held captive by a stronger force. (For example, when American soldiers liberated/redeemed the prisoners in German labor and death camps after WWII.)

- To remove from grave danger or dire circumstances. (For example, rescuers would redeem/free people trapped in the rubble at the World Trade Centre in New York.)

- To acquit someone of a crime. (For example, O.J. Simpson was redeemed from the charge of murder when the jury found him not guilty. The jury's action freed him.)

The basic concept of redemption is that it describes the setting free of someone or something. The redemption theme runs throughout the Bible.

Old Testament Example of Redemption

God rescued/freed/liberated/redeemed the Israelites from Egyptian slavery. The way that God redeemed, or set them free, was through the mighty deeds He did through Moses (Exodus 3:2-10). This freedom or redemption meant three things:

1. Actual freedom from physical slavery to the Egyptians.

2. A new identity for them as people of God (Exodus 3:7).

3. A new purpose in life which would be to "know God."

The idea of redemption is not just a New Testament concept. It appears throughout the Bible from the Garden of Eden to Christ. Every time God freed His people from danger, enslavement and sin He was reinforcing the idea that He was man's redeemer.

New Testament Example of Redemption

In the New Testament the idea of redemption is centered on God's work of freeing mankind, not from human slavery or physical threat, but rather from the enslavement of sin and the resulting penalty of death.

Jesus answered them, "Truly, truly, I say to you, everyone who commits sin is the slave of sin.
- John 8:34

Whoever sins is a slave of sin. Once we begin we cannot stop sinning. We can limit it, keep it down, but we cannot eliminate sin from our lives

> for all have sinned and fall short of the glory of God,
> - Romans 3:23

Everyone sins. There are no exceptions. Everyone is guilty and faces judgment and condemnation.

> For the wages of sin is death, but the free gift of God is eternal life in Christ Jesus our Lord.
> - Romans 6:23

The final outcome of sin is eternal separation from God. God deals with our enslavement to sin and the punishment we face by setting us free. He sets us free, or redeems us, through the atonement of Christ.

> [6] For while we were still helpless, at the right time Christ died for the ungodly. [7] For one will hardly die for a righteous man; though perhaps for the good man someone would dare even to die. [8] But God demonstrates His own love toward us, in that while we were yet sinners, Christ died for us. [9] Much more then, having now been justified by His blood, we shall be saved from the wrath of God through Him. [10] For if while we were enemies we were reconciled to God through the death of His Son, much more, having been reconciled, we shall be saved by His life. [11] And not only this, but we also exult in God through our Lord Jesus Christ, through whom we have now received the reconciliation.
> - Romans 5:6-11

We owe a moral debt to God because we disobey His laws. We cannot pay this moral debt because it requires something we do not have to offer: a sinless life. Jesus, therefore, pays our moral debt for us by offering His perfect life on the cross. This "atonement" pays our moral debt to God forever and permits Him to free us (redeem us) from the prison of guilt and condemnation.

We can express this idea in various ways: The atonement of Christ sets us free; it redeems us; it permits our redemption.

As in the case with the Israelites in the Old Testament, this new freedom/redemption means three very specific things for us.

[11] For the grace of God has appeared, bringing salvation to all men, [12] instructing us to deny ungodliness and worldly desires and to live sensibly, righteously and godly in the present age, [13] looking for the blessed hope and the appearing of the glory of our great God and Savior, Christ Jesus, [14] who gave Himself for us to redeem us from every lawless deed, and to purify for Himself a people for His own possession, zealous for good deeds.
- Titus 2:11-14

1. We are released from slavery
(verses 11; 14[a])

Because we are forgiven and are under God's grace and possess the Holy Spirit, we no longer are slaves to sin. We are not perfect, but we are gaining many more victories over sin and are no longer worried about condemnation because we have been acquitted. Whether O.J. Simpson committed murder or not, the courts can no longer try and condemn him for this crime, he has been acquitted. We have the same experience; we can no longer be condemned for our sins because we have been redeemed/acquitted by the atoning cross of Christ.

2. We have a new identity (verse 14^b)

We are no longer condemned sinners in God's eyes; we are a purified people, a people zealous to do God's will. Redemption transforms us into the people "of God."

3. We have a new purpose (verses 12-13)

Our purpose and direction is heavenward. Our purpose in life is to be ready for the return of Christ by living faithful lives and being busy in the Lord's service.

And so, redemption is the net result of Christ's atoning work on the cross.

Conditions of Our Freedom

This freedom or redemption Christ obtains for us has certain features also explained in the New Testament.

What are we free from?

Redemption frees us from specific things:

1. Freedom from the fear of death and the illusion that this world is all that there is, which seduces us to live only for the here and now.

> ^{14} Therefore, since the children share in flesh and blood, He Himself likewise also partook of the

> same, that through death He might render powerless him who had the power of death, that is, the devil, [15] and might free those who through fear of death were subject to slavery all their lives.
> - Hebrews 2:14-15

2. Freedom from the condemnation that results from judgment. Those who are redeemed are not judged but are acquitted, and so are not subject to condemnation and punishment.

> Therefore there is now no condemnation for those who are in Christ Jesus.
> - Romans 8:1

3. Freedom from eternal death. Those who are redeemed will be fitted with a new body that will live forever.

> For the wages of sin is death, but the free gift of God is eternal life in Christ Jesus our Lord.
> - Romans 6:23

These are some of the things that we are freed or redeemed from through the atonement of Christ.

What are we not free from?

Redemption does not free us from every negative experience. For example, we are not freed from:

1. The physical effects of death that come upon everyone whether they are redeemed or not.

> And inasmuch as it is appointed for men to die

once and after this comes judgment,
- Hebrews 9:27

2. The general effect of sin in our lives, such as guilt, anguish, and regret. We are set free from the spiritual consequences of sin but not necessarily from the physical ones. The thief on the cross still died there. Paul the Apostle still felt anguish for his former persecution of the church.

It is a trustworthy statement, deserving full acceptance, that Christ Jesus came into the world to save sinners, among whom I am foremost of all.
- I Timothy 1:15

3. Temptation and failure. The redeemed still stumble and fall into sin, but they have protection and a promise that their souls are safe despite this.

[8] If we say that we have no sin, we are deceiving ourselves and the truth is not in us. [9] If we confess our sins, He is faithful and righteous to forgive us our sins and to cleanse us from all unrighteousness.
- I John 1:8-9

Redemption is a state that impacts our souls and guarantees our future with God even if our physical lives continue to experience the power and effect of sin.

When This Freedom Begins

There is a moment in time when our personal freedom takes effect. Just as the prisoner released from prison can tell you the date he was set free, the Bible describes the exact moment each soul experiences redemption.

The atonement of Christ was devised by God before time began, but it occurred as an historical event when Christ died on the cross. We can fix a day and time when the atonement took place: the cross. We can fix a day and time when God furnished proof that the atonement was valid, that it worked, that the sacrifice for sin was accepted: the resurrection.

In the same way, the Bible provides an exact moment when redemption happens for us: baptism.

The New Testament uses different words and images to express this, but it always makes the same point: man is free from sin and eternal death at the moment of baptism.

> He who has believed and has been baptized shall be saved; but he who has disbelieved shall be condemned.
> - Mark 16:16

Refers to freedom as being "saved."

> Jesus answered and said to him, "Truly, truly, I say to you, unless one is born again he cannot see the kingdom of God."
> - John 3:3

Refers to freedom as being "born again."

> Peter said to them, "Repent, and each of you be
> baptized in the name of Jesus Christ for the
> forgiveness of your sins; and you will receive the
> gift of the Holy Spirit.
> - Acts 2:38

Describes redemption in terms of forgiveness and the
indwelling of the Holy Spirit.

> Now why do you delay? Get up and be baptized,
> and wash away your sins, calling on His name.'
> - Acts 22:16

Refers to this freedom as a cleansing from sin.

> For you are all sons of God through faith in Christ
> Jesus.
> - Galatians 3:26

Describes this phenomenon as putting on Christ.

> Corresponding to that, baptism now saves you—
> not the removal of dirt from the flesh, but an
> appeal to God for a good conscience—through
> the resurrection of Jesus Christ,
> - I Peter 3:21

Says that redemption is an appeal and granting of a
clear conscience.

The Bible uses many terms to describe this redemption,
this freedom, this liberation, but uses the same moment

and act to pinpoint when this redemption occurs: baptism.

When a person believes that Jesus is the Son of God and has died to atone for his sins; when a person acts on this belief by repenting of his sins and being buried in the water of baptism, at that very moment he or she has redemption. This happens only one time, and does not happen before or after, but only at baptism. You are never any more redeemed or free than on the day and the moment you are baptized.

What Are You Free to Do Now?

People freed from threats of death or prison usually go back to their old life or try to take new directions that will help them avoid being imprisoned again.

Peter explains the lifestyle of one who has experienced redemption and is now free as well as empowered to follow a godly lifestyle.

> [4] For by these He has granted to us His precious and magnificent promises, so that by them you may become partakers of the divine nature, having escaped the corruption that is in the world by lust. [5] Now for this very reason also, applying all diligence, in your faith supply moral excellence, and in your moral excellence, knowledge, [6] and in your knowledge, self-control, and in your self-control, perseverance, and in your perseverance, godliness, [7] and in your godliness, brotherly kindness, and in your brotherly kindness, love. [8] For if these qualities are yours and are increasing, they render you neither useless nor unfruitful in the true knowledge of our Lord Jesus Christ. [9] For he who lacks these qualities is blind or short-

sighted, having forgotten his purification from his former sins. [10] Therefore, brethren, be all the more diligent to make certain about His calling and choosing you; for as long as you practice these things, you will never stumble; [11] for in this way the entrance into the eternal kingdom of our Lord and Savior Jesus Christ will be abundantly supplied to you.
- II Peter 1:4-11

This is the activity and direction of a spiritual life freed from sin by Christ. What Peter explains here is the substance of the "born again" life and what it actually looks like to the outside observer. This is what people do who have been redeemed by Christ's atonement.

We are freed from the prison of sin and now live like free men and women, not free to do as we want, but free and empowered to do what God wants us to do. This is the only true freedom.

Summary

Redemption is the doctrine that explains what man receives as a result of Christ's atoning sacrifice on the cross. In a word: freedom.

Ten words or less that describe the first four sub-doctrines of reconciliation (election, predestination, atonement, redemption): "God foreknew that the atonement of Christ would redeem believers."

MAJOR CHRISTIAN DOCTRINES

I. Inspiration of the Bible
II. Divinity of Christ
III. Original Goodness
IV. Fall of Man
V. Reconciliation
    A. Election ⎫
    B. Predestination ⎪
    C. Atonement   **Plan of Salvation**
    D. Redemption ⎪
    E. Regeneration ⎭

Chapter 10: A New Life in Christ

CHAPTER 10
A NEW LIFE IN CHRIST

The five major doctrines that include the scope of God's dealings with man are:

I.   The doctrine of the inspiration of the Bible.

II.   The doctrine of the divinity of Christ.

III.   The doctrine of the original goodness of man.

IV.   The doctrine of the fall of man.

V.   The doctrine of the reconciliation of man.

I have explained that there are ten sub-doctrines that discuss the process of this reconciliation. The first four of these are:

A. Election: God chooses Christ to be the Savior of mankind.

B. Predestination: God's knowledge that His choice of Christ will achieve His goal, that is, to reconcile man to Himself.

C. Atonement: The method God uses, Christ as a payment for sin.

D. Redemption: What atonement obtains for man, freedom from sin and death.

Once a person is freed from sin and death he can begin a new life. This new life is referred to as regeneration, and is the fifth sub-doctrine that we will study.

Background of Regeneration

The word regeneration itself

> He saved us, not on the basis of deeds which we have done in righteousness, but according to His mercy, by the washing of regeneration and renewing by the Holy Spirit,
> - Titus 3:5

The word "regeneration" literally means, "to make alive again," something that was, was not, then is once again. It comes from the combination of two words: born and again.

We therefore can say, "atonement permits a spiritually dead person the freedom to become spiritually alive again."

Old Testament imagery of regeneration

The restoration of the Jewish people from slavery and exile, and the rebuilding of the Temple in Jerusalem upon their return there are Old Testament examples of God regenerating His people and renewing the practice of their religion.

New Testament imagery of regeneration

> [3] Jesus answered and said to him, "Truly, truly, I say to you, unless one is born again he cannot see the kingdom of God."
>
> [4] Nicodemus said to Him, "How can a man be born when he is old? He cannot enter a second time into his mother's womb and be born, can he?" [5] Jesus answered, "Truly, truly, I say to you, unless one is born of water and the Spirit he cannot enter into the kingdom of God. [6] That which is born of the flesh is flesh, and that which is born of the Spirit is spirit. [7] Do not be amazed that I said to you, 'You must be born again.'
> - John 3:3-7

"Born again," is a term that signifies that a person has an initial birth and eventually experiences a re-birth. One is alive, dead, and then made alive again.

> [16] Do you not know that when you present yourselves to someone as slaves for obedience, you are slaves of the one whom you obey, either

of sin resulting in death, or of obedience resulting in righteousness? [17] But thanks be to God that though you were slaves of sin, you became obedient from the heart to that form of teaching to which you were committed,
- Romans 6:16-17

"Slaves of sin... freedom from sin." One goes from slavery to freedom. Regeneration in this case sees one going from freedom to enslavement and then back to freedom.

For you have not received a spirit of slavery leading to fear again, but you have received a spirit of adoption as sons by which we cry out, "Abba! Father!"
- Romans 8:15

"Sons who cry out Abba, Father." Regeneration here means a change of status from stranger to son. One begins as one's child, becomes a stranger and then returns as a son.

Therefore if anyone is in Christ, he is a new creature; the old things passed away; behold, new things have come.
- II Corinthians 5:17

"New man in Christ." A person is transformed from being an old man to becoming a new man. The process begins as one is created, becomes old with sin and death, and is then regenerated as a new man through Christ.

for you were formerly darkness, but now you are

Light in the Lord; walk as children of Light
- Ephesians 5:8

"Kingdom of darkness... to kingdom of light." The change is from a place of darkness to a place of light. We begin in light, fall into darkness and through the redeeming power of Christ's sacrifice are regenerated to live in the light once again.

In the New Testament the concept of regeneration is expressed as something that was and then was not for some reason, and then is brought back by God's intervention.

The Gospel and Regeneration

The basic message of the gospel/good news is that regeneration is now possible for all. The gospel describes the regenerative process as a "before and after" picture with the redemptive work of Christ's atoning sacrifice in between.

Romans 5:6-11 explains how these doctrines fit together:

[6] For while we were still helpless, at the right time Christ died for the ungodly. [7] For one will hardly die for a righteous man; though perhaps for the good man someone would dare even to die. [8] But God demonstrates His own love toward us, in that while we were yet sinners, Christ died for us. [9] Much more then, having now been justified by His blood, we shall be saved from the wrath of God through Him. [10] For if while we were enemies we were reconciled to God through the death of His Son, much more, having been reconciled, we

shall be saved by His life. [11] And not only this, but we also exult in God through our Lord Jesus Christ, through whom we have now received the reconciliation.

Before:

Sin causes guilt, fear, condemnation, despair and spiritual as well as physical death with no hope of heaven. Some, because of their beliefs or superstitions, may have a false hope of some kind in a paradise or existence after death, but this hope is not one based on the sureness that the witnessed resurrection of Christ provides.

Atoning act on the cross

Jesus pays the moral debt for sin with His sacrifice on behalf of all men for all time.

After:

A response of faith to the cross of Christ produces freedom from the fear of judgment, condemnation and death. This faith also results in a sure hope and peace of mind that in turn leads to the first true experience of what the Bible refers to as "eternal life."

Regeneration and transformation

The doctrine of regeneration describes the transformation that takes place when a person has been freed from sin and its consequences by the atoning work of Christ on the cross.

Regeneration is not something that we do, it is something that happens to us as a result of the redemption/freedom obtained for us by Jesus through His death on the cross. What He does purchases our freedom; our freedom allows us to be regenerated.

For example, a baby does not give itself life. Being born is the result of the actions of others. In the same way, the doctrine of regeneration explains what happens to a person when he or she is born-again as a result of the freedom obtained through the death of Christ on the cross, not as a result of anything we do.

Regeneration details the changes that take place as a person goes from being dead in disbelief and sin to becoming alive through faith in Christ.

Regeneration is usually explained using comparisons to demonstrate the differences between the old and new:

- Lost to saved - Mark 16:16
- Condemned to forgiven - Acts 2:38
- Sinner to saint - Romans 1:7
- Outsider to insider - Galatians 3:20
- Unrighteous to righteous - I John 1:7-9
- Dead to alive - John 3:5

Being a son, being forgiven, being a saint, being saved, etc., these are not things you do, these are things you are, that you have become as a result of your union with Christ. When you become these things it means that you have been transformed or regenerated.

Born-again is a good term because it describes a totally new and different experience of life not experienced or known before.

There is no such thing as a "born-again Christian." Christians are born again as an experience; you are born-again because you are a Christian. The term "born-again" used in this way then, is redundant.

The "Life Signs" of Regeneration

The changes created and described by regeneration cannot be seen. You cannot see forgiveness; sainthood or salvation just like you cannot "see" the wind. However, just as the wind can be seen in what it produces (waves, trees swaying), regeneration is seen in what it produces in the life of the believer.

The new life, the born-again life has a quality, a character that can be seen by others, and in this way proves that regeneration has taken place. I call these regenerative characteristics "life-signs." Just as a person gives signs of life to show that he is alive and well, a born-again/regenerated person also has life signs to show that he or she is spiritually alive as well. Here are a few examples of these "life-signs."

A zeal for the person of Christ

Regeneration puts Christ at the center of one's life. A good example is Paul the Apostle who, after being converted, was entirely focused on preaching the message of regeneration.

> [19] Now for several days he was with the disciples who were at Damascus, [20] and immediately he began to proclaim Jesus in the synagogues,

> saying, "He is the Son of God." [21] All those
> hearing him continued to be amazed, and were
> saying, "Is this not he who in Jerusalem destroyed
> those who called on this name, and who had
> come here for the purpose of bringing them bound
> before the chief priests?" [22] But Saul kept
> increasing in strength and confounding the Jews
> who lived at Damascus by proving that this Jesus
> is the Christ.
> - Acts 9:19-22

Newborns are close to their mother, they cling to the one who gave birth to them. It is the same with Christians, those who are regenerated by Christ want to stay close to Him, feed on Him, please Him and know Him.

A zeal for the Church of Christ

In Acts 2:42 we see how new Christians were engrossed in their life in the body of Christ.

> They were continually devoting themselves to the
> apostles' teaching and to fellowship, to the
> breaking of bread and to prayer.

Those born-again into God's family delight in the activities of that family which include worship and study, fellowship and service. You cannot have zeal for the head of the body (Christ) without zeal for the body (church) as well.

A zeal for the purity of Christ

> [18] Many also of those who had believed kept

coming, confessing and disclosing their practices. [19] And many of those who practiced magic brought their books together and began burning them in the sight of everyone; and they counted up the price of them and found it fifty thousand pieces of silver.
- Acts 19:18-19

The regenerated state brings with it a repugnance of evil, a strong desire to do away with sin in one's life. Born-again people hate their own sinfulness and agonize over the continued evil still present in their flesh.

Paul cried out with the plea of every regenerated person faced with his own sinful flesh when he said, "Oh wretched man that I am, who can save me from this body of sin?" (Romans 7:24)

This experience serves only to heighten their awareness of and appreciation for the atoning work of Christ on the cross. Regenerated people do not rejoice over their sins; however, their sins do help them to see how much they need Christ and to appreciate His sacrifice for them. Although painful at times, this realization causes joy.

Regenerated people cannot be perfect because of their sinful flesh, but they have a great desire to be perfect, and they know that this hunger and thirst for righteousness will one day be satisfied not only through the eyes of faith but in actual fact as well.

A zeal for the works of Christ

Regenerated people have a great desire to do God's work in order to demonstrate their gratitude for their new life and thus, give God glory. Jesus said, "My food is to do the will of Him who sent Me, and to accomplish His work" (John 4:34). Jesus was eager to do God's work, and so are the people who are born-again through His sacrifice.

The zeal that regenerated people have to do God's work, for doing what is right, for knowing and following Jesus, is not a burden. It is a natural characteristic of the born-again spirit, and is the easiest way to separate those who are dead in Christ from those who are alive in Him.

For the outside world of non-believers these are the signs that point out the differences between those born-again and those who are not. The ones I have mentioned are not the only signs of regeneration but are common to those who have experienced the regenerative power of Christ.

The Point of Regeneration

It is obvious that in regeneration we go from being one thing to being another. There is also a point where we cease being lost and become saved, cease being condemned and become forgiven, sinner to saint, etc. Many ask," What is that point?"

Until we get to regeneration, the process of reconciliation is strictly the plan and activity of God. God chooses, God knows, God in Christ pays the price, God's work opens the door to freedom, but at this point man's will enters the picture.

Through the gospel God now offers to man a new life (regeneration) and man is free and able to accept it or reject it. The deciding point, dividing point, transformation point is faith expressed in repentance and baptism. For example, a baby is conceived, matured, carried, but is not born until it comes out of its mother's body. In the same way, a person's faith is conceived, it grows, feelings of repentance emerge, a sense of spirituality develops, but he is not born-again until he comes out of the waters of baptism.

> [3] Jesus answered and said to him, "Truly, truly, I say to you, unless one is born again he cannot see the kingdom of God."

> [4] Nicodemus said to Him, "How can a man be born when he is old? He cannot enter a second time into his mother's womb and be born, can he?" [5] Jesus answered, "Truly, truly, I say to you, unless one is born of water and the Spirit he cannot enter into the kingdom of God.
> - John 3:3-5

Rebirth and baptism are linked together.

> [3] Or do you not know that all of us who have been baptized into Christ Jesus have been baptized into His death? [4] Therefore we have been buried with Him through baptism into death, so that as Christ was raised from the dead through the glory of the Father, so we too might walk in newness of life.
> - Romans 6:3-4

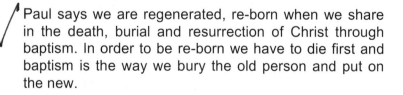

Paul says we are regenerated, re-born when we share in the death, burial and resurrection of Christ through baptism. In order to be re-born we have to die first and baptism is the way we bury the old person and put on the new.

154

> [11] and in Him you were also circumcised with a circumcision made without hands, in the removal of the body of the flesh by the circumcision of Christ; [12] having been buried with Him in baptism, in which you were also raised up with Him through faith in the working of God, who raised Him from the dead. [13] When you were dead in your transgressions and the uncircumcision of your flesh, He made you alive together with Him, having forgiven us all our transgressions,
> - Colossians 2:11-13

A transfer from death to life takes place at baptism because at baptism sins that bring death are forgiven, and we receive the means (the Holy Spirit) to live the regenerated life.

> [5] He saved us, not on the basis of deeds which we have done in righteousness, but according to His mercy, by the washing of regeneration and renewing by the Holy Spirit, [6] whom He poured out upon us richly through Jesus Christ our Savior, [7] so that being justified by His grace we would be made heirs according to the hope of eternal life.
> - Titus 3:5-7

The cleansing and the renewal of our spirit by the Holy Spirit takes place at baptism.

In conclusion, we can say that God chooses His Son to die in order to open the gates of freedom from sin and death which will allow us a new life manifested in zeal for Him, His children and His work. We come into this new life when we express our faith in Christ by burying our old lives in the waters of baptism and resurrect with new lives in Christ.

Summary

God always knew that the atonement of Christ would free believers to experience new lives.

MAJOR CHRISTIAN DOCTRINES

I. Inspiration of the Bible
II. Divinity of Christ
III. Original Goodness
IV. Fall of Man
V. Reconciliation
    A. Election
    B. Predestination
    C. Atonement   **Plan of**
    D. Redemption   **Salvation**
    E. Regeneration

    F. Adoption

Chapter 11: Becoming Children of God

CHAPTER 11
BECOMING
CHILDREN OF GOD

We have been studying the fifth great doctrine of the Bible which is the doctrine of reconciliation. This doctrine has been explained in the following way: God, in His mercy, devised a plan that would reconcile man back to Himself. This plan or process of reconciliation is explained in the Bible using 10 sub-doctrines. So far we have studied five of these:

A. Election: God chooses Christ.

B. Predestination: God knows that His choice of Christ will succeed in reconciling men to Himself.

C. Atonement: God pays the moral debt man owed for sin through the death of Christ on the cross.

D. Redemption: God frees man because the debt for sin is paid for.

E. Regeneration: God breathes new life into the freed sinner.

Now these five sub-doctrines taken together are "God's plan of salvation." Our faith, repentance, confession of Christ, baptism; these are not the plan of salvation. These things are man's proper response to God's plan to save us. Many people confuse the two when trying to preach the gospel to someone.

We need to remember the true context for biblical information when sharing with another:

A. The story of the gospel

This is the actual historical story of Jesus, His life, ministry, death, burial and resurrection (I Corinthians 15:1-5). People need these basic facts in order to establish the true object of faith (Christ) and witness for the power of God (resurrection).

B. The meaning of the gospel

This is God's plan to reconcile man to Himself through Christ. The meaning behind the gospel story is laid out in the doctrines or teachings that explain the gospel message. These doctrines explain why Christ came, what He accomplished and how we are affected. (This is what we have studied until now: reconciliation and the explanatory sub-doctrines).

C. The response to the gospel

God requires man to respond to Him, to Christ, to the good news. This response is described in terms of faith expressed in the actions of repentance, baptism and holy living. So when you are teaching about baptism, you are not proclaiming the story of the gospel or what it means, you are explaining how to respond correctly to the gospel message from God.

Let us get back to our five sub-doctrines. I have said that these first five doctrines explain what God has done, His "plan" to save and reconcile mankind to Himself. Now, the next five sub-doctrines are interesting in that they do not add any more information about reconciliation. The purpose of the next five sub-doctrines is to describe God's plan of salvation from five different perspectives. For example,

F. Adoption: God's plan seen from a human perspective.

G. Justification: God's plan seen from a legal perspective.

H. Perfection: God's plan seen from a heavenly perspective.

I. Sanctification: God's plan seen from an inward perspective.

J. Salvation: God's plan seen from an eschatological perspective. (What it looks like when it is completed.)

In this chapter we begin with the doctrine of adoption and look at God's plan of salvation from a human perspective.

Background

Old Testament ideas of adoption

The main idea or image of adoption in the Old Testament is expressed in God's adoption of Israel as His special child.

> Then you shall say to Pharaoh, 'Thus says the Lord, "Israel is My son, My firstborn."
> - Exodus 4:22

When we examine relationships that people have with God in the Bible we see that only Jesus shares God's divine nature as God, the Son. Only Jesus is referred to as the "only begotten" of God.

On the other hand, mortal men and the nation of Israel, were said to be adopted by God for a special purpose. In describing the sub-doctrine of atonement and explaining the genealogy of Jesus I said that God chose Abraham and his descendants, the Jews, to be His adopted sons. He did this for these people so His only begotten Son, Jesus, would have a physical and cultural heritage and identity when He entered the stage of human history in order to complete His work of atonement on the cross.

New Testament ideas of adoption

In the New Testament the idea of adoption to describe God's plan for reconciliation appears only in the writings of Paul the Apostle (Romans 8:15-23; 9:4; Galatians 4:5; Ephesians 1:5).

He writes about adoption from the Greek and Roman concept of the word and practice. We better understand Paul's point in his description of reconciliation from the perspective of adoption if we are familiar with Greek and Roman adoptive customs.

The basic definition of adoption at that time was:

A legal process by which a man might bring into his family, and endow with privileges of a son, one who was not by nature his son or kindred.

Some of the social and legal customs of the time:

- In Roman and Greek societies, the father had absolute legal power over his children as well as his slaves, wives and property.

- Adoption was not considered a benevolent act. Girls were rarely adopted. Adoptions were done primarily to continue the family line and, at times, an adult male was adopted while his natural parents were alive in order to fulfill a son's role in another family.

- When a male child was adopted, however, he was considered a full son and enjoyed equal rights and privileges of natural sons.

- Roman custom called for a public transaction and a legal ceremony to take place in order for an adoption to be complete. In the case of a child taken out of one family and into another, a ceremony signaled the severing of ties with one family and the adoption into another. As far as the natural family giving up the boy was concerned, the ceremony was the point where they ceased having any relationship with their child.

And so when Paul describes God's plan to reconcile mankind to Himself, he compares it to an adoption process, a very human experience that his readers at the time could easily understand and relate to.

Concept of Adoption in Paul's Writings

There are several passages where Paul explains God's plan using the image of adoption.

> He predestined us to adoption as sons through Jesus Christ to Himself, according to the kind intention of His will,
> - Ephesians 1:5

Here Paul explains in human terms the end result of God's plan. Those separated from Him by sin would ultimately become His children, His sons again through the process of adoption. The end result of His plan was that we would be reconciled as sons and daughters.

> [23] But before faith came, we were kept in custody under the law, being shut up to the faith which was later to be revealed. [24] Therefore the Law has become our tutor to lead us to Christ, so that we may be justified by faith. [25] But now that faith has come, we are no longer under a tutor. [26] For you are all sons of God through faith in Christ Jesus. [27] For all of you who were baptized into Christ have clothed yourselves with Christ. [28] There is neither Jew nor Greek, there is neither slave nor free man, there is neither male nor female; for you

are all one in Christ Jesus. [29] And if you belong to Christ, then you are Abraham's descendants, heirs according to promise. [1] Now I say, as long as the heir is a child, he does not differ at all from a slave although he is owner of everything, [2] but he is under guardians and managers until the date set by the father. [3] So also we, while we were children, were held in bondage under the elemental things of the world. [4] But when the fullness of the time came, God sent forth His Son, born of a woman, born under the Law, [5] so that He might redeem those who were under the Law, that we might receive the adoption as sons. [6] Because you are sons, God has sent forth the Spirit of His Son into our hearts, crying, "Abba! Father!" [7] Therefore you are no longer a slave, but a son; and if a son, then an heir through God.
- Galatians 3:23-4:7

Again in this passage Paul explains the relationship between God's plan and its results. He does this by making a comparison between two types of slavery (4:1).

- In those days, you could be a slave to a master who gave you no rights or freedoms until you could somehow purchase your freedom or be adopted by your master as a son (this was done but happened rarely).

- On the other hand, you could be the young son in a family and as such would be like a slave, completely under your father's rule, until at his discretion you were released through a formal transaction and became legally independent.

The point he makes in this passage is that both child and slave long for the time they can be free to enjoy the privileges of an adult son. Paul says that it is this desire in people (to be sons and daughters of God again) that God responds to with His plan of reconciliation.

No matter who you are (slave, free; male, female; Jew, Greek) the end result is that you share the same sonship/adoption through the reconciling work of Christ. This passage did not mean that these people no longer had their sexual or cultural identities and roles; it explained that their relationship with God had changed.

> [15] For you have not received a spirit of slavery leading to fear again, but you have received a spirit of adoption as sons by which we cry out, "Abba! Father!" [16] The Spirit Himself testifies with our spirit that we are children of God, [17] and if children, heirs also, heirs of God and fellow heirs with Christ, if indeed we suffer with Him so that we may also be glorified with Him.
> - Romans 8:15-17

Here, Paul describes the nature of this adoption. In the Roman world the adopted son was legitimized through a legal procedure. A seal or certificate was made and given to authenticate one's new position within the family. Similarly, God's plan is to have man fully integrated back into fellowship with Him by putting into man the presence of God's Holy Spirit.

Those who become God's sons and daughters through His plan resulting in adoption know and are sure of their new status because they have been "legitimized" in several ways:

- They have been sealed with God's Holy Spirit (Acts 2:38, Ephesians 1:33).

- They call upon God as their own personal Father (Romans 8:15-16).

- They are like God's natural Son, Jesus, in that they share His past (suffering and death) and they share in His future (resurrection and glory) (Romans 8:17).

> who are Israelites, to whom belongs the adoption as sons, and the glory and the covenants and the giving of the Law and the temple service and the promises,
> - Romans 9:4

Paul refers to the fact that this has always been the end purpose of God (to adopt sinners as sons). He explains that it was first promised to the Jews, but they refused His plan (reconciliation through Christ) to achieve it. The Jews thought (and still do to this day) that they were legitimate sons of God through culture and genealogy. And so, in these passages Paul explains the very human experience of adoption as a reference to demonstrate one of the things God's plan of reconciliation does for mankind. In the end God's plan permits lost children to be adopted by a loving Father.

Summary

Let us summarize the information we have so far:

- The doctrines of original goodness and the fall explain how mankind had become lost and helpless orphans separated from God.

- The doctrine of reconciliation has 10 sub-doctrines and the first five of these explain God's plan to remove the sin that separated mankind from Himself.

- The sixth sub-doctrine explains that one result of this plan is that sinful man has been adopted by God to be His child.

One last point about adoption in the first century: in the Roman era, children who were deformed or ill, or adult candidates for adoption who were convicted of crimes were unadoptable. In the same way, we were unadoptable by God because of our sinfulness and imperfection. The imperfect could not become a member of the perfect family. And so, before our adoption could be completed, our imperfections caused by sin and our condemnation as guilty sinners had to be set aside; and this was done through God's plan:

- He knew Christ would succeed: predestination.

- Christ paid the debt for our sins: atonement.

- Once our debts were paid we were freed from condemnation: redemption.

- Now that we are free, God gives us a new life to live: regeneration.

- Once we are free and alive we are qualified to become part of God's family: adoption.

The adopted child in the Roman world had a new home, family, life style and future. The child adopted by God has:

- A new status as a child of God (Galatians 3:26).

- The Holy Spirit within (Acts 2:38).

- The fellowship of other godly children (Acts 2:46).

- A new style of life (holy) (I Peter 1:13).

- An inheritance and wealth which is indestructible and beyond worldly value (Ephesians 1:3).

A summary of the first six doctrines in 10 words: "God promised that Christ's atonement would produce legitimate spiritual children."

MAJOR CHRISTIAN DOCTRINES

I. Inspiration of the Bible
II. Divinity of Christ
III. Original Goodness
IV. Fall of Man
V. Reconciliation
    A. Election ⎫
    B. Predestination ⎪ **Plan of**
    C. Atonement ⎬ **Salvation**
    D. Redemption ⎪
    E. Regeneration ⎭

    F. Adoption
    G. Justification

Chapter 12: Becoming acceptable to God.

CHAPTER 12
BECOMING ACCEPTABLE TO GOD

Through sin man becomes separated from God the Father and thus becomes orphaned. The doctrine of adoption describes how God has adopted us back to being His sons and daughters. Once the thing separating us (sin) has been taken away by Christ's sacrifice, we become free. This freedom comes with a new life breathed into us by the Holy Spirit. As free and spiritually living beings, we are now worthy to be adopted by God to become His sons and daughters.

In this chapter we will look at the doctrine of justification and how this doctrine explains God's plan from the perspective of legality and justice.

Background

Justification as a doctrine is based primarily on the idea that God is the final judge of what is ultimately right or wrong, good or bad. For example, the creation remained neutral until God proclaimed that it was "very good" (Genesis 1:31). The commandments given in Exodus 20:1-ff codified the standards that God established so that the Jews would know without a doubt what was good or bad, acceptable or not. What this means is that God has a right to judge because He has the wisdom to establish the rules and the power to enforce the rules. (i.e. In a democracy the people give the government this right.)

With God, however, the ability to establish, enforce and judge is based on His absolute wisdom and power (we do not give Him authority by consensus). God does not give up any of this authority, but He does reveal in His Word what are His standards, and guarantees that He will enforce them in judgment.

> [5] But because of your stubbornness and unrepentant heart you are storing up wrath for yourself in the day of wrath and revelation of the righteous judgment of God, [6] who will render to each person according to his deeds: [7] to those who by perseverance in doing good seek for glory and honor and immortality, eternal life; [8] but to those who are selfishly ambitious and do not obey the truth, but obey unrighteousness, wrath and indignation.
> - Romans 2:5-8

In this context we begin our study of the sub-doctrine of justification.

To understand justification, we must first understand that it is explained against the backdrop of an absolute standard of what is right and wrong, established by an all-powerful God who will judge the entire world against the standard that He has established. This is the ultimate reality proclaimed by the gospel and espoused by Christians.

The problem today is that many people promote the idea that there is no absolute standard, in the Bible or anywhere. For some, right or wrong is what is right or wrong for you personally. The 9/11 bombing in New York City has had a sobering effect on these people because they cannot condemn this act without violating their personal philosophy about the relativism of morality.

Until recently it has been challenging to preach the gospel because people refuse to accept the absolute nature of God's standard. If there is no standard, then there is no judgment; if there is no judgment then there is no need for salvation. The 9/11 attack, however, showed the weakness of this thinking because America justified its response based on the notion that what was done was morally wrong, and there needed to be a judgment and punishment as a result.

This new awakening to the presence of absolute standards helps us press the case for the gospel and also clarifies the meaning of the doctrine of justification.

A Personal Need

In this context of absolute standards, we begin to understand that one of man's greatest needs is the knowledge and assurance that he lives up to God's standards and thus, God's approval. We have learned that sin deprives us of God's approval because it causes us to live below His standard. This situation causes fear, guilt, anger and despair because we are created to be happy when we obey, and unhappy when we do not.

Those deprived of God's approval but not conscious of it still suffer the symptoms of a soul separated from God and will suffer the final consequences brought on by this condition.

- Now – anxiety, fear, dread

- At judgment – condemnation, punishment

Some believe that ignorance of these things will save these people at the judgment. The Bible, however, says that ignorance is present within men's hearts because they purposefully suppress the very truth that would guide them to God, if they would let it.

[18] For the wrath of God is revealed from heaven against all ungodliness and unrighteousness of men who suppress the truth in unrighteousness, [19] because that which is known about God is evident within them; for God made it evident to them. [20] For since the creation of the world His invisible attributes, His eternal power and divine nature, have been clearly seen, being understood through what has been made, so that they are without excuse. [21] For even though they knew God, they did not honor Him as God or give thanks, but they became futile in their speculations, and their foolish heart was darkened. [22] Professing to be wise, they became fools, [23] and exchanged the glory of the incorruptible God for an image in the form of corruptible man and of birds and four-footed animals and crawling creatures
- Romans 1:18-23

No one is saved by default because they do not know the truth. The Bible says that everyone can know, but willingly suppresses this knowledge.

In addition to this the Bible also claims that even those people who do know the truth (that they do not measure up to the standards of God) are helpless to change this sad reality.

> [18] For I know that nothing good dwells in me, that is, in my flesh; for the willing is present in me, but the doing of the good is not. [19] For the good that I want, I do not do, but I practice the very evil that I do not want.
> - Romans 7:18-19

> [9] What then? Are we better than they? Not at all; for we have already charged that both Jews and Greeks are all under sin; [10] as it is written, "There is none righteous, not even one; [23] for all have sinned and fall short of the glory of God,
> - Romans 3:9-10, 23

This, then, is the cruel paradox of human sinfulness: if you do not know the truth, you are condemned; if you do know the truth, you are powerless to save yourself and remain condemned. This is the problem that the doctrine of justification addresses in explaining God's plan of salvation.

Methods of Justifying Oneself

Man needs God's approval to be at peace with himself and with God. The problem is how to regain this approval, how to measure up to God's standard and become acceptable to Him once again?

Throughout history there have been various attempts to meet this fundamental need:

Man's ways to justify man

Man has invented various ways to deal with his inadequacy before God.

1. Primitive sacrificial system

Giving something (produce, animals, children) to satisfy the anger or appetites of the gods.

Let us not confuse this with the Jewish sacrificial system which God used for a limited time to prepare the Jews for Christ's coming and ministry. They understood that their system merely represented their expressions of thanks, repentance, joy and hope.

> [3] But in those sacrifices there is a reminder of sins year by year. [4] For it is impossible for the blood of bulls and goats to take away sins.
> - Hebrews 10:3-4

The Gentiles, on the other hand, offered sacrifices thinking that their actions actually manipulated the gods for their personal advantage. Primitive religions saw their sacrificial system as a way of making peace with their gods.

2. Law keeping

The most familiar example of this is the Jews. Some, not all, but some Jews believed (and still do) that the way to be acceptable before God is to keep the ceremonial/moral Law. Of course, the version of the Law that they "kept" was very different than what was given to Moses. They watered down the moral Law to suit their purpose and manipulated the ceremonial Law to their liking so that in their minds they were obeying the Law perfectly. Jesus exposed their hypocrisy when He said in Matthew 5:27-28 that adultery began in the heart, not just if someone actually had sex with another man's wife, as they had interpreted it.

They understood correctly that if you obeyed the Law perfectly, you would be acceptable before God, but they did not correctly perceive how demanding God's Law was.

This form of self-justification was also present in the early church as some teachers began to teach a form of ascetic Christianity where people were required to adhere to strict food laws or prohibitions about marriage that God had not required. Paul rebuked these teachers and this false method of making oneself acceptable before God in the epistle to the Colossians.

It is interesting to note that every other major religion that supports the idea of an absolute code of right and wrong (Islam, Judaism, etc.) teaches in one form or another the principle of law keeping as the way to justify or make oneself acceptable to God.

- Islam: pilgrimages, death in war.

- Hinduism: improve your behavior in an ongoing cycle of reincarnated lives.

Even among Christian sects like the Mormons or the Jehovah Witnesses the way to become acceptable is to know and obey the tenets and leaders of the sect itself.

(What makes you acceptable is that you belong to the sect.)

True New Testament Christianity is unique in the religious world because it is the only religion that does not use a form of "law keeping" or conduct based philosophy in explaining how believers are made acceptable before God.

3. Human philosophy

For those who felt the destructive force of sin but suppressed the truth of God's existence, the way of dealing with man's imperfection was through godless philosophy. The ancient philosophers sought for higher levels of understanding and wisdom through efforts at meditation and logic that continued through the ages. The thought was that the more that man knew and understood, the better he became.

4. Magic

Magic and occult practitioners try to control the unseen world for the improvement of their lives using physical means such as charms and rituals.

These various efforts have led to the most recent stage of Western Post Modernism where people have given up trying to be better and settled for simply accepting themselves as they actually are. In this way they do not have to justify themselves to anyone, including God. They create their own standard and change it when it does not suit them anymore.

God's way to justify man

Human beings can find many ways to justify and make themselves acceptable, but in order to be acceptable before almighty God, we must do this His way, using His method. In His Word, God not only reveals His absolute standards and His judgment on those that do not meet His standards, He also reveals the time and method that He has set forth for all men and women to become justified and therefore acceptable before Him. This is what the doctrine of justification explains, the time and method for man to become acceptable before God.

1. The time is now!

We do not become acceptable before we are born, after we die, after suffering in purgatory, or after we have completed so many acts in this life or several lifetimes; the time is always now.

> for He says, "At the acceptable time I listened to you, And on the day of salvation I helped you."
> Behold, now is "the acceptable time," behold, now is "the day of salvation".
> - II Corinthians 6:2

The time to become right with God is not when we know more, or when we feel more perfect or holy, when we feel worthy or spiritual. It is not on our birthday or on some other anniversary. The time to become acceptable to God is when we discover how He wants us to do it. When we discover how, then the moment is now!

2. The method is by imputation

The method is not by sacrifice or law keeping or philosophy. It is by imputation.

The word impute means to consider or to put something onto someone else. For example, an "honorary" college degree is valid and given without the person taking the necessary courses: the title "doctor" is imputed or put upon someone without him actually earning that privilege through his academic efforts.

In God's plan of salvation, He has sent Christ to live up to His perfect standard and actually earn the title of human perfection. Jesus earned acceptability by perfectly obeying God's Law exactly as it was written and meant to be obeyed.

That perfection, that acceptable status is conferred or imputed or put upon us (like an honorary degree) when we are united to Christ by faith. We cannot earn this status; it is imputed to us.

Romans 3:19-24 explains the process.

> [19] Now we know that whatever the Law says, it speaks to those who are under the Law, so that every mouth may be closed and all the world may become accountable to God; [20] because by the works of the Law no flesh will be justified in His sight; for through the Law comes the knowledge of sin.

God's standard/Law speaks to all. The principle of law (the absolute standard which is God's Law) will be what all men are judged by.

The Jews had a special revelation of God's standard through Moses, but everyone has had some form of exposure to it: through creation which is outward revelation, or through conscience which is inward revelation.

The purpose of giving the Law was not only to establish a standard, it was also to show men their true condition as sinners. Just as a thermometer does not produce heat or cold but only measures it, God's Law did not produce good or bad, it measured the sinfulness of man and exposed it to judgment.

> [21] But now apart from the Law the righteousness of God has been manifested, being witnessed by the Law and the Prophets,

God has demonstrated in a person, not just a written set of rules, what is acceptable and perfect. When this person was compared to the standard, He was found perfect.

> [22] even the righteousness of God through faith in Jesus Christ for all those who believe; for there is no distinction; [23] for all have sinned and fall short of the glory of God, [24] being justified as a gift by His grace through the redemption which is in Christ Jesus;

This quality of perfection, acceptability, some call it righteousness, is now imputed/conferred/transferred upon all who believe in Him. This action of imputing Christ's perfection upon believers is done by God freely, as a demonstration of His kindness. This is the only way and the only method that a person can be justified or made acceptable before God.

Summary

The doctrine of justification explains how God's plan of salvation solves the problem of making men who are helplessly trapped in the imperfection of sin, perfect and acceptable again through Christ. This is what we mean when we say that we are "justified" (made acceptable to God's standard) through faith in Jesus Christ (His perfection is imputed to us when we are united to Him by faith).

Paul combines the moment with the method in Galatians 3:26-27:

> [26] For you are all sons of God through faith in Christ Jesus. [27] For all of you who were baptized into Christ have clothed yourselves with Christ.

We are united to Christ by faith at the moment of baptism; we are justified or made acceptable when through the method of imputation, God clothes us with Christ's perfection in baptism. This is the heart and soul of the gospel message.

The seven sub-doctrines in 10 words or less: God knew believers would become His acceptable children through Christ.

MAJOR CHRISTIAN DOCTRINES

I. Inspiration of the Bible
II. Divinity of Christ
III. Original Goodness
IV. Fall of Man
V. Reconciliation
    A. Election ⎤
    B. Predestination ⎥
    C. Atonement ⎬ **Plan of Salvation**
    D. Redemption ⎥
    E. Regeneration ⎦

    F. Adoption
    G. Justification
    H. Perfection

Chapter 13: God's New Vision of Mankind

CHAPTER 13
GOD'S NEW VISION OF MANKIND

Let us start with a little review from our last chapter. Two ways of being acceptable/justified before God:

1. Man's way – primitive sacrificial system, law keeping, philosophy, magic.

2. God's way – time: now (I Corinthians 6:2), method: imputation (Romans 3:19-24).

The doctrine of justification says that we are justified when we become acceptable to God according to His standard. We become acceptable when God confers/imputes "acceptability" upon us based on our faith in Jesus Christ. God confers this acceptability upon us when we express our faith in Christ at baptism.

> [26] For you are all sons of God through faith in Christ Jesus. [27] For all of you who were baptized into Christ have clothed yourselves with Christ.
> - Galatians 3:26-27

We are justified by faith; we express faith through repentance and baptism.

God's plan was that Jesus would live up to God's standard and thus earn an acceptable standing before God so that He could share this status with those who believed in Him. Justification describes God's plan from a legal perspective, how we relate to God through the Law.

In this chapter we will look at God's plan from a heavenly perspective and see what God's plan has done to change God's view of us. In other words, because of Jesus, God now sees us in a different light and the doctrine of perfection explains this new way God sees us.

General Definition

The doctrine of perfection describes the quality of the condition of those who are in Christ. For example, a hospital patient has a condition: hospitalized; the quality of his condition: critical, stable, etc.

The dictionary describes perfection as something that is entirely without flaw or defect; something that satisfies all the requirements.

The biblical concept, however, is different. The Old Testament used the term "perfect" to denote healthiness, completeness, wholeheartedness; but not sinless perfection. For example, fruit is perfect when it is ripe and fully developed, not if it is without blemishes.

> Let your heart therefore be wholly devoted to the Lord our God, to walk in His statutes and to keep His commandments, as at this day.
> - I Kings 8:61

Here the writer says that one must not waiver in faith; he does not mean that a person will never sin.

The New Testament follows the same pattern. The word perfect and the idea of perfection suggest wholeness, ripeness, full-grown, maturity.

> [27] to whom God willed to make known what is the riches of the glory of this mystery among the Gentiles, which is Christ in you, the hope of glory. [28] We proclaim Him, admonishing every man and teaching every man with all wisdom, so that we may present every man complete in Christ.
> - Colossians 1:27-28

Spiritual perfection/completeness/maturity can be pursued in many ways, but we can only reach wholeness and spiritual ripeness through Christ.

A major deviation in this teaching came through John Wesley (Methodist Church) who taught that "perfection" in the New Testament meant sinless perfection now in this lifetime. His doctrine was largely due to the influence of a book he was reading at the time called, "A Practical Treatise on Christian Perfection" by William Law. Wesley argued that after regeneration/rebirth a man had the ability to actually overcome any sin.

Although it is true that with the new birth comes the ability to overcome sin in our lives, the danger in overemphasizing this fact is that we may lose sight of God's plan whereby Christ has successfully dealt with all of our sins on the cross once and for all as far as our salvation is concerned. If we see the doctrine of perfection as a teaching that says, "in order to be perfect we must overcome every sin in our lives," then we have misunderstood. If this is what we understand by the doctrine of perfection, then we will be locked back into a works oriented salvation leading to frustration and discouragement.

- We all sin (Romans 3:23).

- We will always sin (I John 1:1-10).

- No one is able to become perfect by sinless law keeping (Romans 3:20). Not that we would not like to be, we just cannot. Therefore, we have to find another way to be perfect, and the doctrine of perfection explains how.

The question is, "How do we become perfect, ripe, whole, mature when we continue to experience the failure of sin in our lives?" The doctrine of perfection explains how God's plan has achieved this status for us in Christ. Paul explains it in detail in Philippians 3:4-16.

Paul's Explanation of Perfection

[4] although I myself might have confidence even in the flesh. If anyone else has a mind to put confidence in the flesh, I far more: [5] circumcised the eighth day, of the nation of Israel, of the tribe of Benjamin, a Hebrew of Hebrews; as to the Law, a Pharisee; [6] as to zeal, a persecutor of the church; as to the righteousness which is in the

Law, found blameless.

Here the Apostle reviews everything that in every culture and generation represents the perfect man: right culture, spiritually superior and advanced, religious zealot, clear conscience (acceptable before God through law keeping).

> [7] But whatever things were gain to me, those things I have counted as loss for the sake of Christ. [8] More than that, I count all things to be loss in view of the surpassing value of knowing Christ Jesus my Lord, for whom I have suffered the loss of all things, and count them but rubbish so that I may gain Christ,

Paul explains that whatever things he had which could be measured to achieve perfection before no longer count now that he has come to know Christ. He thought he was perfect before but now that he has faith in Christ and knows Christ, he realizes that he did not even know what perfect meant. The way he is perfect (spiritually ripened, mature) through faith in Christ is far superior to the perfection he thought he had through his culture, zeal and previous law keeping.

> [9] and may be found in Him, not having a righteousness of my own derived from the Law, but that which is through faith in Christ, the righteousness which comes from God on the basis of faith,

God establishing a way to have a union with Christ through faith is the thing that makes one perfect/mature in His eyes, not law keeping. This is the core of the doctrine of perfection.

> [10] that I may know Him and the power of His resurrection and the fellowship of His sufferings, being conformed to His death; [11] in order that I may attain to the resurrection from the dead.

The result of this perfection based on faith in Christ is that we will be resurrected from the dead as He was. I may lose the status of perfection based on worldly criteria, I may even die for this faith, but it is worth it because it is this faith in Christ that signals my perfect spiritual state in God's eyes.

Someone may ask, "Why struggle against sin if faith in Christ is what makes you perfect in God's eyes?" The answer is that slavery to sin is a denial of one's faith in Christ, and one's struggle against sin is a continuing expression of that faith.

The greater the struggle, the greater the love and faith. Peter says, "...he who has suffered in the flesh has ceased from sin" (I Peter 4:1). This does not mean that the person never sins, rather that the person no longer loves sin, lives for sin; now he lives for Christ, loves righteousness, etc.

Paul Looks Ahead

> [12] Not that I have already obtained it or have already become perfect, but I press on so that I may lay hold of that for which also I was laid hold of by Christ Jesus.

Paul explains that he has not obtained the fruit or the results that comes from being in this mature/perfect state. It may be confusing here because he refers to the results or final effects of perfection by lumping them in with the status of perfection itself. He is referring to the things that come as a result of being in the perfect or mature state in Christ, things that only "spiritually perfect" people can hope for.

Paul mentions two things that his perfect status before God permits him to strive for:

1. Resurrection: this will only happen after he dies.

2. Glorification: this will only happen when Christ returns and he is transformed into the actual likeness of Christ.

These are the dual goals that God originally called Paul (and us) for through the gospel. Paul presses forward to the goals set before him by God and made possible by the perfection he enjoys in Christ.

- One day he will die and resurrect in order to put on a glorified body suitable for existence in the spiritual world.

- That body will be perfectly matched with the character of Christ interposed upon his own.

Paul consciously pursues these goals and encourages his readers to do the same because only "perfect" people can try for these. (i.e. Only Olympic athletes can go for Olympic medals.)

> [13] Brethren, I do not regard myself as having laid hold of it yet; but one thing I do: forgetting what lies behind and reaching forward to what lies ahead, [14] I press on toward the goal for the prize

of the upward call of God in Christ Jesus.

The method to reach these begins by forgetting the past. Put aside both failures (which are covered by the blood of Christ), and successes (which cannot achieve the perfection he needs to enable him to obtain his goals). Paul strives forward to be in Christ through faithful obedience, like Christ through submission, and with Christ through resurrection.

> [15] Let us therefore, as many as are perfect, have this attitude; and if in anything you have a different attitude, God will reveal that also to you; [16] however, let us keep living by that same standard to which we have attained.

Here Paul addresses those Christians who understand that their perfection is accomplished/made possible through continued faith in Christ, not self-achievement or rule keeping. He says to these people that they should follow his example, and his example is that he presses on! He does not look back at past failures, past mistakes, past sins. He does not excuse, condemn or congratulate himself. He looks ahead at the goal God has set for him and all those like him. Paul tells his readers that if this is what they are doing, then they are doing the right thing, striving for the right goals.

He also realizes that not everyone may be on the same spiritual level; some are only beginning in Christ, others are eager to move forward and still others are unsure of their status.

Paul tells them not to worry if they have different ideas on these matters or unanswered questions and doubts. God will eventually lead them into maturity and into the confidence that perfection brings. In the meantime, they are to maintain this teaching as the standard for the understanding of what "perfect" is and is not.

Perfection is attained through faith and not through law keeping. He tells his readers to be patient until this doctrine is learned. This is a fundamental concept of the gospel and if one does not know or understand this, it can hinder all other spiritual growth and peace of mind.

Summary

The doctrine of perfection explains that in this life we reach the ultimate state of spiritual completeness when we are united to Christ by faith.

We do not and cannot achieve perfection by overcoming every sin in our lives. Sinless perfection is granted us when we are fitted with a glorified body after resurrection. Until then we enjoy that status based on our faith in Christ and we demonstrate that faith in our daily struggle against sin, not our perfect victory over sin. Christ has already won that victory for us with His life, His death on the cross and His glorious resurrection.

Here is a summary of the main biblical doctrines and eight sub-doctrines under reconciliation in 10 words or less: God always knew that Jesus' sacrifice would perfect His children.

MAJOR CHRISTIAN DOCTRINES

I. Inspiration of the Bible
II. Divinity of Christ
III. Original Goodness
IV. Fall of Man
V. Reconciliation
    A. Election
    B. Predestination
    C. Atonement   **Plan of**
    D. Redemption   **Salvation**
    E. Regeneration

    F. Adoption
    G. Justification
    H. Perfection
    I. Sanctification

Chapter 14: How Mankind Becomes Holy

CHAPTER 14
HOW MANKIND BECOMES HOLY

In this chapter we are going to look at the doctrine of sanctification, the view of God's plan from the inward perspective. Sanctification is the doctrine that explains how God devised a plan to enable man to share in His holiness.

Sanctification – Word Meaning

There is no English word to directly translate the biblical idea of sanctification. The English word is a transliteration of two Latin words: *sanctus* (holy) and *facere* (to make). The meaning of the basic Hebrew and Greek words was to set apart, or in some instances to be bright, or brightness as in light brightness.

In the Old Testament any person or thing set apart by God for His personal use was considered sanctified.

Common things, places and people took on a special value by virtue of their being chosen by God for His purpose. This is why many people use the word "sanctuary" for the meeting room where the church conducts public worship to God. That place/space has been set apart/sanctified for a special purpose in the service of God. This is one of the reasons why some are sensitive about using it for other purposes not connected to worship (social events or recreation in a multipurpose setting).

In the Bible, being "set apart" or "sanctified" for a specific purpose or task meant that a new quality of life was expected from those who were consecrated (another way of saying set apart or sanctified). The terms and conditions of this new life and purpose were established by the one who was doing the setting aside, in this case God.

Sanctification – Action

In the process of sanctification, it is always the greater who sets aside the lessor. Military generals set aside lower ranked soldiers for certain positions and duties, not vice versa. The greater the superiority of the one setting aside, the more significant the consecration of the one being set apart. For example, being appointed teacher representative by the principal is not as great an honor as being appointed teacher of the year by the governor of the state, or voted in as city manager by the city council versus being appointed secretary of state by the president of the nation.

From a major Christian doctrine perspective, consider the greatness of the one who separates us from the world in order to now live in Christ. The One who consecrates us is:

The Creator of the world

[1] In the beginning God created the heavens and the earth. [2] The earth was formless and void, and darkness was over the surface of the deep, and the Spirit of God was moving over the surface of the waters. [3] Then God said, "Let there be light"; and there was light.

- Genesis 1:1-3

A perfectly holy and eternal being

For thus says the high and exalted One
Who lives forever, whose name is Holy,
"I dwell on a high and holy place,
 And also with the contrite and lowly of spirit
In order to revive the spirit of the lowly
And to revive the heart of the contrite.

- Isaiah 57:15

If this is the position of the One who does the setting apart/the sanctifying, imagine the quality of life to which those who are set apart are called?

Sanctification – Nature

So we understand what sanctification is: a setting apart for a purpose. We understand who does it: God Himself through Christ and His Word. But what is this sanctified state like?

In the Old Testament we could follow the clearly marked changes of those who were set apart for the priesthood. They received special garments to wear and were given instruction as to their lifestyle and their work in the temple. What are the changes for those who are set apart in Christ?

The Old Testament priesthood prefigured this future sanctification of believers in Christ. Their sanctification was carried out on an external basis (clothes, work, lifestyle); a Christian's sanctification is carried out on an inward basis.

In this context the doctrine of sanctification, therefore, explains two things:

1. The new status of those reconciled.

Christians have been called out of the world by the gospel and set apart in Christ.

> [26] For you are all sons of God through faith in Christ Jesus. [27] For all of you who were baptized into Christ have clothed yourselves with Christ. [28] There is neither Jew nor Greek, there is neither slave nor free man, there is neither male nor female; for you are all one in Christ Jesus.
> - Galatians 3:26-28

Christians were "in" the world, the world of sin, disbelief and death. Now they have been taken out of the world through faith and set apart or consecrated to Christ. Our old status was that of sinners condemned to die, our new status is that of saints separated to live in union with other believers in the body of Christ, the church.

This new status includes all of the blessings described in the previous doctrines as aliveness, freedom, perfection and sonship. These are some of the features of our new status in Christ.

Sanctification also explains:

2. The new purpose of those reconciled.

The Old Testament priests were set aside with a new status that enabled them to fulfill a new purpose: the servants of the temple and of the sacrificial system. The new purpose of Christians is to manifest Christ to the world.

> [14] You are the light of the world... [16] Let your light shine before men in such a way that they may see your good works, and glorify your Father who is in heaven.
> - Matthew 5:14, 16

This is the purpose for which we were set apart or sanctified in Christ. All that we do serves this purpose in one way or another. Therefore, the sub-doctrine of sanctification explains the new status (in Christ) and purpose (to manifest Christ) of the Christian set apart by God.

In the Old Testament the priests' sanctification addressed mainly the outward appearance and tasks of these men; in the New Testament the Christian's sanctification is spiritual in nature and affects the inward man.

Sanctification – Common Errors

As with many of the doctrines we have studied, there have been errors that have been taught concerning the doctrine of sanctification. One of the most common ones has to do with the way of identifying those who have been sanctified. For example:

Those sanctified have spiritual gifts

Many groups believe that the sure sign that one has been sanctified is their ability to speak in tongues. There were many gifts mentioned in the Bible, but this is the one most referred to in the last 100 years. The Bible however, describes this gift as the ability to speak in "known" languages...

> ^{3} And there appeared to them tongues as of fire distributing themselves, and they rested on each one of them. ^{4} And they were all filled with the Holy Spirit and began to speak with other tongues, as the Spirit was giving them utterance.
>
> ^{5} Now there were Jews living in Jerusalem, devout men from every nation under heaven.^{6} And when this sound occurred, the crowd came together, and were bewildered because each one of them was hearing them speak in his own language. ^{7} They were amazed and astonished, saying, "Why, are not all these who are speaking Galileans? ^{8} And how is it that we each hear them in our own language to which we were born?
> - Acts 2:3-8

...and that with time this gift would cease.

> Love never fails; but if there are gifts of prophecy, they will be done away; if there are tongues, they will cease; if there is knowledge, it will be done away.
> - I Corinthians 13:8

What is put forth today does not resemble at all what the Bible describes as speaking in tongues, and even if it were, would not be the definitive proof of sanctification.

Those sanctified can perform miracles

Again this idea is proposed by some who think that the proof that they have been set apart by God for ministry is their ability to do miracles. The problem here is that most faith healers' ability to cure is based on the disease and the relative faith of their followers, and there is always a money factor in the process.

In the Bible those who had this ability could heal anyone of anything, even raise the dead. They did not have to be near or touch the person (Peter and Paul healing people whose handkerchief was brought forth or if their shadow crossed the sick person's path, Acts 5:15). And there was never any question of failure or money attached to their healing ministry. Timothy and Titus were mighty servants as were Luke, Mark and Silas, but none of them performed miracles.

So to say that a sign, calling or sanctification unto ministry in the modern era is demonstrated by miraculous power is not biblical.

How do we know that we are truly sanctified?

Those who have been set apart by God into Christ know that this is the case in the following ways:

By faith

The Word teaches that those who repent, believe and are baptized will be forgiven, will receive the Holy Spirit, will be transferred from the world to the body of Christ, and now belong to the kingdom of light (Mark 16:16, Acts 2:38, Galatians 3:26, Colossians 1:13).

We know we are sanctified in the same way we know everything else about our reconciliation: by faith. We believe God's Word when He promises that those who believe in His Son and express their faith in obedience will be sanctified.

By power

Not the external power to do miracles and signs, but by the internal power that enables us to manifest Christ to the world.

> [9] For this reason also, since the day we heard of it, we have not ceased to pray for you and to ask that you may be filled with the knowledge of His will in all spiritual wisdom and understanding, [10] so that you will walk in a manner worthy of the Lord, to please Him in all respects, bearing fruit in every good work and increasing in the knowledge of God; [11] strengthened with all power, according to His glorious might, for the attaining of all steadfastness and patience; joyously [12] giving thanks to the Father, who has qualified us to share in the inheritance of the saints in Light,
> - Colossians 1:9-12

In these verses Paul describes the experience of sanctification:

- Knowledge of God's will
- Spiritual wisdom, understanding
- Obedience to His Word
- Fruitfulness in good works
- Ever deepening relationship with God in prayer and assurance
- Ability to persevere
- Joyful and thankful heart
- Hope of eternal life in heaven

Sanctification is a spiritual state whereby we become holy like God, we take on the character of Christ and manifest it to the world:

- Adoption describes our new relationship with God.

- Justification describes our new standing with God.

- Perfection describes the new quality that God gives us.

- Sanctification describes the new character that God is developing in us, and moving us to manifest to the world.

Adoption, justification and perfection happen in a moment (at baptism) when we are united to Christ through faith; these cannot be increased by any other activity. Sanctification, however, is a process that takes place throughout our lives and will be completed when we receive our glorified bodies at the return of Christ.

> [50] Now I say this, brethren, that flesh and blood cannot inherit the kingdom of God; nor does the perishable inherit the imperishable. [51] Behold, I tell you a mystery; we will not all sleep, but we will all be changed, [52] in a moment, in the twinkling of an eye, at the last trumpet; for the trumpet will sound, and the dead will be raised imperishable, and we will be changed.
> - I Corinthians 15:50-52

At that time, we will manifest perfect obedience, wisdom, knowledge, strength, etc.

The Process of Sanctification

I said that adoption, justification and perfection happen at the same moment (at baptism), but sanctification is a process that takes time. Warren Wiersbe, in his book, "Be Ready" says that there are three changes/stages in the process of sanctification:

1. Positional Stage

This is when we are actually set apart by God into our new position in Christ at baptism. This is the beginning stage (Hebrews 10:10).

2. Practical Stage

The practical stage is experienced in every Christian's daily effort to manifest Christ to an unbelieving world (II Corinthians 7:1). Of course God helps in this daily struggle and effort. Unlike the priests, He does not give us special uniforms, rules and job descriptions. He provides: the Holy Spirit (Romans 8:2), the Word (II Timothy 3:16), the church (Ephesians 4:2), and the cross (I John 1:7-9). This stage lasts for as long as we live on this earth.

3. Perfected Stage

When Christ comes we will actually be perfected and actually manifest His perfect likeness for eternity (I John 3:2).

Sanctification says that we are set aside by God to become like His Son, Jesus Christ, as we faithfully struggle each day until He returns and completes our sanctification. We lose our position only if we abandon the practical task of manifesting Christ as best we can each day. So long as we practice manifesting Christ, God assures us that when Christ comes, practice will be turned into perfection.

One of the most common errors that Christians make is that they fail to understand that adoption, justification and perfection all happen in an instant at baptism, and that sanctification is a lifelong process. The error made is that they begin to worry about losing their justification, their adoption, their perfect standing in God's eyes when their daily struggle in the process of sanctification is not going quickly enough or when they have experienced setbacks. Or, they try to earn justification, adoption or perfection by working extra hard in the process of sanctification. In this life you are never more justified (forgiven), adopted (belong to God) or perfect (acceptable) to God as the day you were baptized.

Sanctification is the preparation/fitting for the glorious body we will receive at resurrection. Sanctification is preparation for the heavenly life and the manifestation of that heavenly life to the world now. You do not gain heaven by this process, you experience heaven.

Since sanctification is a process, it also explains a few things that happen in the church. For example:

- Why some people remain saved even though they are extremely immature spiritually. Their immaturity simply shows that they are not far in the process.

- It also explains why we should not be discouraged or afraid when we fail. The process is a long and painful one, and so long as we are willing to remain faithful, God will continue to bring us along.

- It also tells us why we should always have hope for ourselves and others, because God's promise is that one day we will all be exactly like Jesus and manifest Him perfectly to one another.

Think of that brother or sister you dislike or are at odds with, and realize that one day the sin and weakness you dislike will be gone and only Jesus' perfect character will remain. Better to try to love them now than later, that is part of the process.

In closing this chapter let us try to summarize the sub-doctrines we have looked at so far: God promised that those He set apart would perfectly manifest Christ.

MAJOR CHRISTIAN DOCTRINES

I. Inspiration of the Bible
II. Divinity of Christ
III. Original Goodness
IV. Fall of Man
V. Reconciliation
    A. Election
    B. Predestination
    C. Atonement   **Plan of**
    D. Redemption   **Salvation**
    E. Regeneration

    F. Adoption
    G. Justification   **Views of**
    H. Perfection   **the Plan of**
    I. Sanctification   **Salvation**
    J. Salvation

Chapter 15: The Role of Baptism and Communion

CHAPTER 15
THE ROLE OF BAPTISM AND COMMUNION

We are studying the 10 sub-doctrines that explain God's plan to reconcile sinful man back to Himself in an acceptable or righteous state. The first five of these explain how God achieved this reconciliation (the plan of salvation), and the last five describe the outcome of the plan and examine the plan from different perspectives.

The last of these sub-doctrines is called the doctrine of salvation. The word salvation comes from the Greek word (*soteria*) which means deliverance (to rescue or set free). And so, the doctrine of salvation describes the distinction now made between ourselves and others because of God's plan.

> He who has believed and has been baptized shall be saved; but he who has disbelieved shall be condemned.
> - Mark 16:16

We are the rescued, and we are those who are set free. For example, in the movie Titanic we saw that some of the passengers were lost and some were rescued. In the same way, the doctrine of salvation demonstrates a similar reality, some are saved and some are lost.

This last sub-doctrine is the briefest to explain in our series because it is the summary of all the doctrines we have studied so far. Salvation is the doctrine that embodies the entire process whereby through God's plan we become holy, innocent, perfect sons and daughters of God and avoid the terrible consequences of sin.

Salvation is short hand for all that we have studied in this series. For example, the term "The Presidency" includes all the details, authority and duties of the President in one word. In the same way the doctrine of salvation includes the teaching on the creation, fall and reconciliation of man with all of the details contained in the 10 sub-doctrines.

When we say that we are "saved" or we talk about our "salvation," we are saying in a single word everything I have said in this book. It is the final result of God's plan, looking at it from its completion point.

An important teaching that stems from this study is how the actions of baptism and communion fit into the overall teachings of these major doctrines.

Baptism and Major Christian Doctrine

Many times we teach about baptism and we focus mainly on how to do it properly and that it should be performed immediately at belief.

After our study of major doctrines, we are better able to see where baptism fits into the overall picture and context of Christian teaching. After our study in doctrine we should better be able to understand the "what" of baptism (what it is) and the why of this action. In essence, baptism is the historical moment when we receive the benefits derived from God's plan.

Jesus' historical expression of love was made at the cross (John 3:16). We can pinpoint the day, date, hour of this event.

Our historical expression of faith is baptism (Mark 16:16), the expression of faith we make in response to God's offer of rescue and reconciliation.

In Ephesians 4:5, Paul says that there is only one baptism, and he taught this for two important reasons:

1. To distinguish Jesus' baptism from others

In Paul's day there were many types of baptisms being practiced: pagan admission rites, Jewish purification with water, the baptism of John the Baptist. Because of this Paul wanted to impress upon them that only one baptismal/water ritual now counted with God, and that was the immersion in water of repentant believers in relation to Christ and no other.

Someone might ask, "What about Holy Spirit baptism?" The Apostles received this at Pentecost. The sign for this was the tongues of fire that appeared over them (Acts 2:1-3). We receive the indwelling of the Holy Spirit at water baptism (Acts 2:38), and once we have experienced this, there is no other baptism left to administer.

2. To establish its importance

In every passage dealing with baptism, it is always associated with salvation. There was only one Lord, one faith, and one baptism and these three were tied to the salvation offered by God (and I use salvation here in the sense that we've studied it: as the summary of all things produced by God's reconciliation).

When we talk about baptism, we are talking about an interchangeable word that can be used for salvation. The word salvation includes everything we have discussed concerning man's reconciliation. The word and action of baptism embodies all of these same things in actual historical fact and not just in religious theory. When a person is baptized, that person receives in actual fact, not just in theory:

- Christ's elect status as a chosen one of God, explained in the doctrine of election.

- They are subject to God's promise of salvation outlined in the doctrine of predestination.

- They receive payment for their personal sins as the doctrine of atonement explains.

- They are actually set free from the judgment and condemnation they were under as the doctrine of redemption explains.

- They begin to experience the new life given to them by God and detailed in the doctrine of regeneration.

- They actually can call on God as their Father and not before, as the doctrine of adoption says.

216

- These people are now truly and forever innocent and acceptable to God as the doctrine of justification says.

- Baptized people are now, in reality, considered perfect in God's eyes as the doctrine of perfection teaches.

- These believers now live a new and different life with a new and different purpose as the doctrine of sanctification outlines.

- And finally, those who believe and are baptized can say with confidence, without pride or judgment, that they are the saved because that is what the doctrine of salvation teaches.

One Baptism, Many Descriptions of Salvation

The Bible, therefore, teaches that there is only one baptism, that moment in time when an individual is immersed in water because of their faith in Christ as the Son of God and receives salvation and the blessings attached to salvation.

A problem that many have concerns the validity of their baptism and if they should do it over again. There is confusion here because we often fail to realize that in the New Testament the idea of salvation is expressed using different imagery and different terms.

We know that baptism and salvation are related to one another and we know how. The problem lies in the fact that when the Bible writers mentioned the idea of salvation, they did not always use the same words/images. Here are some examples of this phenomenon:

Salvation = Disciples

> [18] And Jesus came up and spoke to them, saying, "All authority has been given to Me in heaven and on earth. [19] Go therefore and make disciples of all the nations, baptizing them in the name of the Father and the Son and the Holy Spirit,
> [20] teaching them to observe all that I commanded you; and lo, I am with you always, even to the end of the age."
> - Matthew 28:18-20

Salvation = Obedience

> He who has believed and has been baptized shall be saved; but he who has disbelieved shall be condemned.
> - Mark 16:16

Salvation = New birth

> Jesus answered, "Truly, truly, I say to you, unless one is born of water and the Spirit he cannot enter into the kingdom of God.
> - John 3:5

Salvation = Forgiveness

> Peter said to them, "Repent, and each of you be baptized in the name of Jesus Christ for the forgiveness of your sins;
> - Acts 2:38a

Salvation = Holy Spirit

and you will receive the gift of the Holy Spirit.
- Acts 2:38b

Salvation = Added to the church

So then, those who had received his word were baptized; and that day there were added about three thousand souls.
- Acts 2:41

Salvation = Burial and resurrection

Or do you not know that all of us who have been baptized into Christ Jesus have been baptized into His death?
- Romans 6:3

Salvation = Adoption

For you are all sons of God through faith in Christ Jesus.
- Galatians 3:26

Salvation = Clothed with Christ

For all of you who were baptized into Christ have clothed yourselves with Christ.
- Galatians 3:27

Salvation = Clear conscience

[20] who once were disobedient, when the patience

of God kept waiting in the days of Noah, during the construction of the ark, in which a few, that is, eight persons, were brought safely through the water. [21] Corresponding to that, baptism now saves you—not the removal of dirt from the flesh, but an appeal to God for a good conscience—through the resurrection of Jesus Christ, [22] who is at the right hand of God, having gone into heaven, after angels and authorities and powers had been subjected to Him.
- I Peter 3:20-22

Note some important features of these 10 scripture references.

1. They all refer to salvation. This is the point that they are making. The passages talk about the issue of salvation in context, and I mean salvation from the doctrinal perspective that we have been discussing as the summary of all the previous doctrines.

2. They each refer to salvation from a different perspective and use different imagery to describe it. To be obedient to God is the same as to be saved; to have a clear conscience before God is the same as being saved. In other words, only a saved person can be a disciple, obedient, born again, forgiven, filled with the Holy Spirit, a member of the church, resurrected with Christ, be a child of God, wear Christ and have a clear conscience. Only saved people have and experience these things!

3. Note that all of these salvation passages include baptism as the dynamic moment when these things take place. You cannot separate baptism

from salvation. No matter how the writers referred to or described salvation, faith was always the constant element, and baptism its physical expression.

Now if we understand this we can answer the four most asked questions that invariably arise when we speak about baptism.

Most Asked Questions About Baptism

1. Is baptism necessary for salvation?

The answer is yes. Only saved people can claim to be obedient to the gospel, can claim to be disciples, can say that they are forgiven, filled with the Holy Spirit, members of the body, etc. Only saved people can claim to have these things and these things are given and come into effect at baptism. Previously, 10 scripture references were listed in order to prove this point.

2. Does the Bible not say we are saved by faith?

Yes, it does, but when it teaches this it is always in response to those who are trying to be saved by a system of law or culture. Salvation has always been by faith, not by perfect law-keeping or belonging to a specific culture (Romans 3:27-30). Faith, however, has always been expressed according to God's will in concrete ways, for example: Noah's faith expressed in building the ark; Moses' faith expressed in returning to Egypt to face Pharaoh; believers in Jesus expressed their faith in repentance and baptism (Acts 2:38).

In the New Testament the writers always contrasted faith versus law, not faith versus baptism. The writers understood that baptism was an act of faith that demonstrated the authenticity of their belief. A person who believed the gospel expressed that faith in repentance and baptism and was thus saved. This is what "obeying the gospel" actually means.

3. What about Romans 10:10-13?

> [10] for with the heart a person believes, resulting in righteousness, and with the mouth he confesses, resulting in salvation. [11] For the Scripture says, "Whoever believes in Him will not be disappointed."

> [12] For there is no distinction between Jew and Greek; for the same Lord is Lord of all, abounding in riches for all who call on Him; [13] for "Whoever will call on the name of the Lord will be saved."

This passage is used by Evangelicals to prove that the "moment" of salvation is when one gives intellectual acceptance, when one thinks or decides to believe, this is the historical moment of salvation, not baptism. The reason they believe this is because they do not interpret this passage in its proper context. I could do the same thing with other passages. For example:

> [46] and He said to them, "Thus it is written, that the Christ would suffer and rise again from the dead the third day, [47] and that repentance for forgiveness of sins would be proclaimed in His name to all the nations, beginning from Jerusalem.
> - Luke 24:46-47

If this were the only passage I used, I could say that repentance was the point of salvation, not faith or baptism.

You have to see the passage in context, what does Romans 10:10-13 mean in context? Let us see what Paul is talking about in Romans:

- Romans chapters 1-3 – All men are guilty of sin.

- Romans chapters 4-5 – God's plan of salvation through reconciliation achieved by Christ.

- Romans chapters 6-8 – The response to God's offer and the terms of this new life in Christ.

- Romans chapters 9-11 – Why the Jews did not believe.

- Romans chapters 12-16 – How to live as Christians in this world.

Romans 10:10-13 is a passage located in the section where Paul is explaining why the Jews, who had great spiritual advantages, failed to receive the promised salvation. Paul is comparing the Gentiles (who did not know God but accepted Jesus), to the Jews (who had the Law, the prophets and the promises but rejected Him). He says that the Jews rejected Jesus because, among other things, they tried to achieve righteousness through law keeping and ritualism, and thought they were succeeding (9:32-10:3).

He goes on to say that the Gentiles, on the other hand, pursued salvation through a system of faith in the Savior, His cross and their response to Him. At this point he quotes from the Old Testament to demonstrate that this idea of "salvation through a system of faith" was known in Old Testament times and was not a new doctrine (as the Jews may have accused him of teaching). This was not new theology; it was taught by the prophets themselves! (Verse 11, Isaiah 28:16 and verse 13, Joel 2:32)

He is explaining the method God uses to save us: faith, not the response to the gospel which is faith expressed in repentance and baptism (Romans 6).

4. Should I be re-baptized?

Many ask this question because they are not sure how to resolve the issue. In Acts 19 we have good information to help us decide this issue. In Acts 19 Paul re-baptized 10 men who had been baptized in the proper way (by immersion) but for the wrong reason (John's baptism of repentance and preparation for the coming of Christ). He explained salvation to them in terms of the Holy Spirit (Acts 2:38) and re-baptized them so they would receive the gift of the Holy Spirit. Now, Paul could have explained salvation using any number of images (sonship, clean conscience, clothed with Christ), but he did not, he chose only one image of salvation and baptized them (forgiveness and the reception of the Holy Spirit - Acts 2:38).

Here are the questions to ask when it comes to rebaptism:

1. Was I baptized the right way?

By immersion in water, as a repentant believer in Christ. If you are not sure that you have done this (if you were sprinkled or poured, etc.), redo your baptism correctly (by immersion).

2. Was I baptized for the right reason?

The reason for baptism is salvation. That salvation could have been explained to you in various ways:

- Baptized to obey the gospel (Mark 16).

- Baptized to become a disciple (Matthew 28).

- Baptized to be born again (John 3).

- Baptized to receive forgiveness and the Holy Spirit (Acts 2:38).

- There are other biblical reasons, but these should suffice for sake of argument.

When you are baptized for one of the ideas connected to salvation, you receive all the blessings of salvation.

For example, when I was baptized in 1977, I did it to obey Christ and be forgiven of my sins. I did not realize at the time that I had also received the Spirit, was clothed with Christ, became Son of God, etc. The Bible teaches that If you have one of these, you have them all.

If, on the other hand, you were baptized for a reason not connected to salvation: to show that you were saved at some other time, to please your parents, to join a particular church, to do it so you could take communion, you are in error. These are not biblical ideas and you should reconsider and restudy the issue.

Biblical Reason + Biblical Method = Biblical Salvation

Major Christian Doctrine and Communion

There is a beautiful fulfillment and dynamic at work when we take the Lord's Supper, because in this action are stitched together all of the doctrines we have spoken of as well. In Acts 2:42, one of the first actions we see the recently baptized converts doing is sharing the Lord's Supper.

Whereas baptism marks the historical moment when we appropriate all the blessings provided for us through God's plan of salvation, communion is a commemoration of God's plan throughout history.

1. The symbols remind us of the plan.

- The choice of Christ, the perfect sacrifice broken for us.

- Death as a payment to bring freedom and life.

2. The common action of eating and drinking remind us of the benefits.

- Innocent, acceptable children, holy before God, eating and drinking with each other.

- This is why communion is taken after baptism and not before.

3. The repetition each Lord's day.

- As a reminder to the world that God's plan will one day be completed when the Lord comes again.

Once again let us try to summarize what we have learned so far in a single thought: Through baptism and communion, God's plan of salvation and man's faith come together in a concrete physical form that blesses man and honors God.

MAJOR CHRISTIAN DOCTRINES

I. Inspiration of the Bible
II. Divinity of Christ
III. Original Goodness
IV. Fall of Man
V. Reconciliation
    A. Election
    B. Predestination
    C. Atonement   }   **Plan of Salvation**
    D. Redemption
    E. Regeneration

    F. Adoption
    G. Justification
    H. Perfection   }   **Views of the Plan of Salvation**
    I. Sanctification
    G. Salvation

VI. Kingdom of God

Chapter 16: The Kingdom of Heaven on Earth

CHAPTER 16
THE KINGDOM OF HEAVEN ON EARTH

If you were to take all of Jesus' sermons and teachings together and study them for a particular style or central theme you would learn that the central theme in His preaching, especially as recorded by Matthew, Mark and Luke, was the idea of the kingdom of God or the kingdom of heaven (He talked about this the most). He spent much time talking about the coming, the preparation for, the nature of and the makeup of the kingdom.

It seems that Matthew used the term kingdom of heaven because the Jews had been trained to think in terms of heaven as a spiritual dimension. Mark uses the term kingdom of God because his Gentile audience could more easily identify with this (they had no idea of heaven).

Jesus used the word kingdom throughout His ministry, and 13 of His 43 parables begin with the words, "The kingdom of heaven is like..." Obviously if Jesus gave so much importance to the subject of the kingdom and our involvement in it, we should be familiar with His teachings on it.

This is why I have included the teaching/doctrine of the kingdom as one of the seven major doctrines of the Bible that explains our faith. We do not have the time to explore all 13 parables that describe the kingdom (for a more complete study on this topic see the video series or book entitled "Kingdom Parables" on the BibleTalk.tv website), but we can review how the doctrine of the kingdom developed over time.

Development of the King and Kingdom: Ideas in the Old Testament

Theocratic Rule

In the beginning society was designed to co-exist in peace with extended families, sharing the limitless resources of a perfectly balanced creation, all under the loving care and presence of God: Genesis. There were no human rules of any kind. The only present authority was God and His Word.

With the advent of sin, a new level of authority was instituted within the family structure in that the husband was to have authority over his wife; but no authority in society yet. After the flood (Genesis 9) God gave society the authority to police itself and execute justice for crimes (a life for a life, Genesis 9:6) in order to provide order in a new sinful world.

The first human ruler was self-appointed. In Genesis 10:10, Nimrod forms and reigns over his own kingdom and was probably the main instigator in building the

Tower of Babel. This is the first instance recorded in the Bible of a human king and kingdom.

The word king is translated from a root word in the Greek which means ruler; and the word kingdom comes from a variation of that word which refers to the geographical area over which that ruler rules.

So the sinful world after the flood had gotten to the point that it had thrown off God's rule and presence, and began to appoint themselves as rulers and kings.

With the selection of Abraham to begin forming a new people who belonged to God, there was a return to family rule with God as guide and protector. As the nation of Israel formed from the 12 tribes descended from Jacob we noted that contrary to pagan nations, the Jews still maintained the tribal leaders as the highest form of authority under the direction of God's influence and presence in their lives. Although they came into contact with pagan kings, the Jews remained without a king for over two centuries after they entered the Promise Land. Up until this time they lived under a theocratic rule; in other words, God was their king and He guided them through the prophets, judges and the Law of Moses.

Human kings

Once settled in their promised land, and while carrying on military campaigns against border enemies, a movement began to select one person to serve as king over the people of Israel. This was against God's will, but nevertheless He permitted the people a change in system and warned them that they would regret it.

The Bible records the sad experience that the Jews had with earthly kings beginning with the first:

- Saul went mad, died in disgrace.

- David was a great king but disobeyed God with terrible sins.

- Solomon built the temple but became unfaithful, leading the nation into idolatry.

- The kingdom was divided into two (North and South) after Solomon's death.

- The Northern Kingdom was totally destroyed for idolatry and evil kings.

- The Southern Kingdom was also destroyed and carried off into exile for the same reason, but allowed to return to Jerusalem and rebuild the city and the temple after 70 years.

- Only a small portion of the Southern Kingdom remained under the rule of Rome when Jesus was born to Mary.

God's Relationship with the Kings

The idea that God is a king or has a kingdom is not apparent in the early portions of the Bible. The image of God's relationship and position with earthly kings and His own stature as king as well as the entire idea of a spiritual kingdom is developed very slowly by the different writers of the Old Testament.

God cannot reveal a concept that people have no way of relating to or understanding. This gradual development of an idea is referred to as progressive revelation. This is where God slowly reveals a concept one step at a time over many years through different writers. His kingship and kingdom are two ideas revealed slowly to mankind.

We know that human kings were subject to God and feared Him (Genesis 20:1-7): Abimelech, King of Shur feared God's wrath when he unknowingly took Abraham's wife into his harem. We also see the Pharaoh resist God's judgment and finally give in when God destroyed the first born in Egypt prior to the Jews being released from captivity.

However, the direct relationship between God and a king begins with Saul, the first king of Israel. In this relationship we see that God chooses and establishes kings. I Samuel 8:5-7 says that although God permits it, He recognizes that the people have chosen a human king instead of remaining with Him as their king. This is the first hint of God as king. Later on there will be a mention that He has a kingdom as well.

The idea that God was a king with a kingdom was introduced into the Jewish mindset over a long period of time.

Man as Divine King

Aside from the concept that God was a king with a kingdom, there existed the idea that a human could be a divine ruler of sorts. The Egyptians may have been the first to combine the idea that the king was a descendant or product of the gods and therefore divine (sun kings). This may have been why Pharaoh was so stubborn seeing Moses as some other descendant of the gods and thus a rival to be defeated.

The Greeks revived this idea for western civilization with Alexander the Great and then the Romans took it over.

Augustus Caesar (63 BC-14 AD) saw his role and person as an incarnation of the gods and thus began emperor worship throughout the empire. When Christians confessed Jesus as Lord (Divine King), this raised up a possible challenge to the Roman order and led to the subsequent persecution of Christianity along with other illegal religions of the era.

The idea of the divine human king did not survive after Rome fell but continued in the East (Shinto, Japan).

In the Jewish world we see the idea of God ruling as a divine king in heavenly places long before the empires of Greece and Rome were formed. David describes God in this rule in Psalms 47:2-3; 101:1.

The earliest direct reference to the title king being used for God is in the 8th century before Christ, by Isaiah the prophet.

[1] In the year of King Uzziah's death I saw the Lord sitting on a throne, lofty and exalted, with the train of His robe filling the temple. [2] Seraphim stood above Him, each having six wings: with two he covered his face, and with two he covered his feet, and with two he flew. [3] And one called out to another and said, "Holy, Holy, Holy, is the Lord of hosts

The whole earth is full of His glory."

[4] And the foundations of the thresholds trembled at the voice of him who called out, while the temple was filling with smoke. [5] Then I said,

"Woe is me, for I am ruined!
Because I am a man of unclean lips,
And I live among a people of unclean lips;

For my eyes have seen the King, the Lord of hosts."
- Isaiah 6:1-5

By this time in the Jewish mind, the idea that God is the king who rules over all kings is firmly fixed. (1200 years from Abraham to Isaiah.)

The New Testament idea of the divine king taking on a human form and dwelling among men and inviting them into His divine kingdom will be processed by several prophets over another eight centuries.

The King and the Kingdom in the New Testament

After Isaiah, the prophets Zechariah and Obadiah began to describe the Messiah as a charismatic ruler (king) who would appear and renew the golden period of Jewish history (Solomon). This leader would rule from Jerusalem, he would purify the nation, he would save it from its enemies, he would have sovereignty over all the nations.

It was this kind of prophecy that stirred the hopes of the nation for a redeemer and savior to come in the future. These prophets filled out the description of the "one to come" spoken of before but not well pictured.

Daniel picks up and develops this image even further in Daniel 7 by giving an exact historical time when this person would come. In Daniel 7 he describes the rise and fall of four world kingdoms and then the establishment of a fifth and final kingdom. Daniel, however, adds two important ideas to the ones already mentioned:

1. The Messiah is a divine king, not just a human ruler.

2. He will rule not only by Himself, but will rule with His people who will constitute a divine kingdom.

The concept of the Messiah as divine king ushering in a special kingdom to rule over all other kingdoms was finally expressed in its fullness by Daniel.

This sets the stage for the last two prophets to speak about the kingdom of God:

John the Baptist

When John comes along, the people are anticipating a king who will purify, save and exalt the Jewish nation over its enemies. John's initial preaching falls in line with their expectations: repent and be baptized to purify yourselves and be ready for the kingdom is coming. The people responded to this recognizable message. John also announced the divine aspect of the kingdom by speaking of the Holy Spirit and how the One to come would baptize the people with Him.

The idea that the king and the kingdom were two different things, and that there would be great political change when he came, caused confusion for both John and the people.

Jesus the Messiah

When Jesus finally arrives, He follows John's preaching about the kingdom but He tells them that the kingdom has arrived. The deduction is that if the kingdom has arrived, then the king (Messiah) is here too. At first, with His miracles and teachings, the people see Him as the king they have imagined coming, but when the political changes do not happen they begin to reject Him and are confused.

Jesus is the one who develops fully the concept of the kingdom only partially described throughout history by the different prophets:

- He explains that the divine king is at the center of the kingdom (not like human kings who are above).

- He explains that the kingdom is not earthly (political), but spiritual in nature.

- He tells them that the kingdom is made up of the king and those who are united to Him by faith, not culture.

- He explains that the kingdom has a:

  o Past – prophesied and hoped for.

  o Present – Jesus manifests its king and provides an earthly dimension for it: the church.

  o Future – at the end of the world all aspects of the kingdom (earthly/ heavenly) will merge into one.

This is where His 13 parables on the kingdom fit in, through them Jesus describes the nature and tension between the present condition of the kingdom and its future consummation when He returns.

The Kingdom Theology in Post New Testament Times

A lot of what we think about the kingdom of God today is based on various theological ideas that were developed after the New Testament was written.

Roman Catholicism – Augustine

Catholic thought, formed by Augustine (4th century), was that the kingdom and the church were exactly the same thing. They saw the kingdom as a spiritual monarchy where the Pope was ordained as head of the church and the church ruled as a kingdom with lesser officials ruling its different parts. This explains why Popes and Cardinals dress like kings or royalty. For Roman Catholics the hierarchy of the kingdom was the feature most stressed in their teaching.

Protestants – Reformers

The Protestant reformers emphasized the spiritual aspects of the kingdom (Luke 17:20, "…The kingdom of God is not coming with signs to be observed"). The kingdom, they taught, was not manifested in a strict hierarchy like the Catholics believed, but in the work of the Holy Spirit among the believers. The transformation of lives was the sign of true believers who inhabit the kingdom. Charismatics carried this idea to the extreme with the display of various "gifts" and ability to "prophesy" as the mark of those who belonged in the kingdom.

Modern Theology

The "Social Gospel" proponents see the kingdom as God's presence in men making the world a better place.

The current Pope, Francis, with his teachings about the poor, the environment, the evils of capitalism, etc. is very much a believer of this image of the kingdom whose role is to make this world a better place.

Of course the task of Christians is to understand and experience the kingdom as Jesus saw and explained it, a more accurate biblical view of the kingdom teaches that:

- Jesus is at the center of the kingdom. It begins and ends with Him.

- The church is its expression here in the physical realm. This is explained in Jesus' parables and Sermon on the Mount.

- The complete fullness of the kingdom will be achieved when Jesus returns to glorify the church/kingdom.

- The kingdom will be fully integrated when God, Christ, the Holy Spirit, the church, the angels and the spiritual world will be united into one unit forever at the end of the world.

The study of the kingdom involves understanding the difference between where we are and how we function now (in the present state of the kingdom of heaven/God here on earth), and where and how we will be when the kingdom is fully realized in the future, when Jesus returns. This is why we study the Sermon on the Mount and Jesus' parables about the kingdom: that is where the information is!

This leads us to the last of the seven major doctrines: doctrine of the second coming, which we will look at in the next chapter.

MAJOR CHRISTIAN DOCTRINES

I. Inspiration of the Bible
II. Divinity of Christ
III. Original Goodness
IV. Fall of Man
V. Reconciliation
    A. Election
    B. Predestination
    C. Atonement   **Plan of**
    D. Redemption   **Salvation**
    E. Regeneration

    F. Adoption
    G. Justification
    H. Perfection   **Views of**
    I. Sanctification   **the Plan of**
    G. Salvation   **Salvation**

VI. Kingdom of God
VII. Second Coming

CHAPTER 17
JESUS DESCRIBES THE END

In our previous chapter about the nature of the kingdom of God I said that Jesus, in His parables and Sermon on the Mount, describes the kingdom and how it operates here on earth. The kingdom being a spiritual entity with Him at the center and those who believe in Him tied together with Jesus and one another by faith.

This kingdom/church functions according to His will and purpose as it awaits its fulfillment when He returns. This fulfillment includes:

- The resurrection and glorification of all the saints.

- The punishment of the wicked.

- The passing away of the present heaven and earth to be replaced with a new heaven and earth.

- The unification of the church and the Godhead into eternity.

Since all of these things are to happen in the twinkling of an eye when Jesus returns (I Corinthians 15:52), it is important that we have an understanding of the end times as taught by Jesus and others. In this chapter we will examine what Jesus taught His disciples concerning His return and the end of the world.

The main teaching by Jesus on this topic is found in Matthew 24-25. He has just rebuked the religious leaders because of their hypocrisy and lack of faith. In Matthew 24 the Lord begins a long and difficult passage describing the end of not only the Jewish nation (which will take place about 40 years into the future), but also the end of the world when He will return.

Discourse on the Judgment

Jesus leaves the temple and as He leaves, the Apostles point out the magnificent buildings of the temple that He has just said will be destroyed. (50 years of reconstruction work was in progress at the time.)

> [1] Jesus came out from the temple and was going away when His disciples came up to point out the temple buildings to Him. [2] And He said to them, "Do you not see all these things? Truly I say to you, not one stone here will be left upon another, which will not be torn down."
> - Matthew 24:1-2

Jesus responds to their comment by saying that the buildings will not only be empty, they will be completely torn down. This sets up further questions by the disciples; Peter, James, John and Andrew wanted more information about what He had just said. They questioned Him about the time when the destruction of the temple would be, and what signs would accompany the second coming and the end of the world which the second coming was to bring.

> As He was sitting on the Mount of Olives, the disciples came to Him privately, saying, "Tell us, when will these things happen, and what will be the sign of Your coming, and of the end of the age?"
> - Matthew 24:3

Whether they thought both these events would happen at the same time or with a lapse of time is unknown, they did not know and were asking Jesus to instruct them in these matters.

This section is complex but can be divided into three major periods for easier explanation:

1. A panoramic view of world history until the second coming of Jesus that includes the destruction of Jerusalem in 70 AD (verses 4-14).

2. A telescopic view to events leading up to and including the destruction of Jerusalem in 70 AD (verses 15-35).

3. A second telescopic view to the second coming of Jesus at the end of the world (verses 36-44).

Panoramic View Until Second Coming (24:4-14)

> [4] And Jesus answered and said to them, "See to it that no one misleads you.

These instructions are given so that they will know and avoid false teachers and prophets in these matters.

> [5] For many will come in My name, saying, 'I am the Christ,' and will mislead many. [6] You will be hearing of wars and rumors of wars. See that you are not frightened, for those things must take place, but that is not yet the end. [7] For nation will rise against nation, and kingdom against kingdom, and in various places there will be famines and earthquakes. [8] But all these things are merely the beginning of birth pangs.

The cycle of false prophets, wars, and troubles in the world will continue until the end, but these in themselves are not the signs; they are only the beginning of things that will get progressively worse before not only the end of Jerusalem comes, but also the end of the world comes.

> [9] "Then they will deliver you to tribulation, and will kill you, and you will be hated by all nations because of My name. [10] At that time many will fall away and will betray one another and hate one another. [11] Many false prophets will arise and will mislead many.
> [12] Because lawlessness is increased, most people's love will grow cold.

This is a parallel to II Thessalonians where Paul talks about the end of the world and what must take place first: an apostasy (a falling away, Christians' love grows cold), the Man of Lawlessness, who deceives many through false signs and tries to take the place of God, will be revealed. In addition to these, Jesus describes the devolution of the world.

> ^{13} But the one who endures to the end, he will be saved.

In contrast He promises that the faithful will be saved despite these trials and evil.

> ^{14} This gospel of the kingdom shall be preached in the whole world as a testimony to all the nations, and then the end will come.

He also promises that the great commission will be carried out and must be carried out before the end can/will come.

This is a panoramic view of the events and flow of history that will occur until His second coming.

Telescopic View to the Fall of Jerusalem
(24:15-35)

Judea was rebellious and longed to return to the glory days of independence and power at the time of Solomon. In 60 AD they had such unrest that Rome sent in troops to quell the rebellion. From 66-70 AD the Roman armies successfully laid siege to Jerusalem and totally destroyed the city and temple along with over one million people. This total destruction of the Jewish nation was the fulfillment of Jesus' prophecy to the disciples 33 years earlier described in this passage. The disciples wanted to know when this would happen and Jesus gives them the "signs" to watch out for.

> [15] "Therefore when you see the abomination of desolation which was spoken of through Daniel the prophet, standing in the holy place (let the reader understand), [16] then those who are in Judea must flee to the mountains. [17] Whoever is on the housetop must not go down to get the things out that are in his house. [18] Whoever is in the field must not turn back to get his cloak.

The first sign was the "abomination of desolation." The point was that when the temple would be desecrated this would be a sign that destruction was near and they should escape the city. Daniel (11:31; 12:11) had prophesied that the temple would be defiled, and it was in the days of the Maccabees (160 BC) by the Syrian King Antiochus Epiphanes who sacrificed a pig on the altar of the temple in Jerusalem.

Jesus picks up this idea and says that in the same way when the temple will be defiled by Gentiles during their lifetimes, it will be the signal to escape.

Luke 21:20 tells us that the surrounding of the temple by foreign armies is what constituted defilement. The standards (shields) of the Roman army were idolatrous and often used for worship by the soldiers, and surrounding the temple with them would desecrate it. Many scholars differ here as to what the abomination was and refer to Jewish historians for events that could fit (events that would have occurred before, during or after the siege). However, Luke 21:20 is the only biblical reference that actually matches the event in context.

"He who reads" means he who reads Daniel and, along with Christ's cryptogram, will be able to know when it is time to get out, and many did. In 68 AD the majority of Christians living in Jerusalem escaped to the city of Pella thus avoiding being killed in the massacre.

> [19] But woe to those who are pregnant and to those who are nursing babies in those days! [20] But pray that your flight will not be in the winter, or on a Sabbath. [21] For then there will be a great tribulation, such as has not occurred since the beginning of the world until now, nor ever will.

The tribulation is the suffering caused by the Romans which wiped out the nation when over one million people were killed. The combination of the gravity of the sin (Jews who received the blessings and promises and ultimately killed their Messiah) and the horror of the punishment (the nation wiped out) has not been equaled.

> [22] Unless those days had been cut short, no life would have been saved; but for the sake of the elect those days will be cut short.

God's providence permitted this war to end so that the Christians would not also be annihilated along with the Jews. Their city was destroyed and Romans made no distinction between Christian and non-Christian Jew at that time.

> [23] Then if anyone says to you, 'Behold, here is the Christ,' or 'There He is,' do not believe him. [24] For

> false Christs and false prophets will arise and will show great signs and wonders, so as to mislead, if possible, even the elect. [25] Behold, I have told you in advance. [26] So if they say to you, 'Behold, He is in the wilderness,' do not go out, or, 'Behold, He is in the inner rooms,' do not believe them.

The believers would naturally associate the destruction of Jerusalem with the return of Jesus, so the Lord warns them against being deceived by those who would claim to be the Lord or speak from God.

Josephus, a Jewish historian of the time, documents how rumors of the Messiah coming or being present circulated in order to keep people in the city. In those days, hysteria and fear produced many "prophets" who claimed visions and messages from God. One fake prophet said that he would separate the Sea of Galilee and 25,000 followed him out.

> [27] For just as the lightning comes from the east and flashes even to the west, so will the coming of the Son of Man be.

He tells them that when He returns it will be evident to all, like lightning across the sky, all will easily and readily know that it is He.

> [28] Wherever the corpse is, there the vultures will gather.

The corpse is the Jewish nation; the vultures are the false Christs and prophets. When you see them in abundance they will be a second sign that the end of "Jerusalem" is near, not the end of the world.

> [29] "But immediately after the tribulation of those days the sun will be darkened, and the moon will not give its light, and the stars will fall from the sky, and the powers of the heavens will be shaken.

The first words "but immediately," in this verse present a problem to some. If we make this next section a discussion about the end of the world and the second coming of Jesus, then it must occur right after the destruction of Jerusalem (some believe and teach Jesus has already returned and promote this idea in a teaching referred to as the 70 AD Theory).

Since the Man of Lawlessness has not been revealed and Jesus has not returned, as Paul teaches concerning the signs of the end of the world in II Thessalonians chapter 2, this passage must still be talking about events surrounding the destruction of Jerusalem.

> [30] And then the sign of the Son of Man will appear in the sky, and then all the tribes of the earth will mourn, and they will see the Son of Man coming on the clouds of the sky with power and great glory. [31] And He will send forth His angels with a great trumpet and they will gather together His elect from the four winds, from one end of the sky to the other.

Therefore, verses 29-31 speak about the destruction of Jerusalem and the effects that this has on non-believers and believers alike. The language is apocalyptic and is used by prophets to describe cataclysmic historical and political events (i.e. Isaiah 13 describing the destruction of Babylon in similar language). Language using the symbolism of the destruction of heavenly bodies is used to describe the very real fate of the world at the end (II Peter 3:10), but also the end and destruction of nations on the earth before the end of time. In this case the end of the Jewish nation as a people under God's special care.

The coming of the Son of Man refers to both the second coming at the end of the world and the final judgment, but also any judgment God makes on any nation, in this case the nation of Israel.

It also fits the context of this passage. The Jews who rejected Him now will see Him coming as a form of judgment on their nation, a terrible catastrophe that would horrify the world, but liberate Christians and the gospel from Jewish persecution.

The Greek word translated "angel" can also be translated as "messenger." This verse can be seen as prophecy concerning the spreading of the gospel throughout the world after the fall of Jerusalem. Verse 14 said this needed to be done before Christ returned, and now with the ideological and cultural restraints of Judaism removed, Christianity would flourish even more.

> [32] "Now learn the parable from the fig tree: when its branch has already become tender and puts forth its leaves, you know that summer is near;
> [33] so, you too, when you see all these things, recognize that He is near, right at the door.
> [34] Truly I say to you, this generation will not pass away until all these things take place. [35] Heaven and earth will pass away, but My words will not pass away.

Jesus warns them to pay attention to the signs He has given them because they will happen in their generation and He promises by His word that they will happen!

Telescope to Second Coming (24:36-44)

Jesus has just explained to them the signs that will preview the destruction of Jerusalem:

- Preaching of gospel to all nations (Romans 10:18)
- Multiplication of false Christs (Josephus)
- Abomination of temple (Luke 21:20)
- Great tribulation (Josephus)

Now in verses 36-44 He contrasts this with the second coming at the end of the world.

> [36] "But of that day and hour no one knows, not even the angels of heaven, nor the Son, but the Father alone.

No one knows the time, not even Jesus. While He was with the disciples He knew when Jerusalem would end, but not the end of the world.

> [37] For the coming of the Son of Man will be just like the days of Noah. [38] For as in those days before the flood they were eating and drinking, marrying and giving in marriage, until the day that Noah entered the ark, [39] and they did not understand until the flood came and took them all away; so will the coming of the Son of Man be.

There will be no cataclysmic signs, all will seem normal; normal in the sense that the believers will be preparing themselves for the second coming and the end of the world while the rest of the world will be ignoring it until it will be too late (just like in the time of Noah).

> [40] Then there will be two men in the field; one will be taken and one will be left. [41] Two women will be grinding at the mill; one will be taken and one will be left.

Some take this verse to mean that before Jesus returns some will be taken in a "rapture" and disappear to be with God in heaven. This is part of the Pre-Millennial view of the rapture and 1000-year reign. In context, however, Jesus is talking about readiness and He says that when He returns suddenly one will be saved, one lost, no time for repentance and change.

Just like Noah, when the rain came they were taken and disappeared into the ark, the others remained to die in the flood. When Jesus comes, the faithful will be taken to be with Him and the disbelievers immediately put away from His presence.

> [42] "Therefore be on the alert, for you do not know which day your Lord is coming. [43] But be sure of this, that if the head of the house had known at what time of the night the thief was coming, he would have been on the alert and would not have allowed his house to be broken into. [44] For this reason you also must be ready; for the Son of Man is coming at an hour when you do not think He will.

Since the end is to be like this we should always be prepared and not foolishly lapse into sin thinking we have plenty of time to repent and be ready for the return; we never know, we must be ready.

Exhortations to Vigilance (24:45-25:30)

After responding to the question of the judgment on Jerusalem and His return, Jesus warns them to be vigilant and does so with three parables.

1. Parable of the evil slave (24:45-51)

Here the lesson is not to presume we have the luxury of sinning because the end is far away, it can come at any time and the judgment is sure for those who are unfaithful.

2. Parable of the 10 virgins (25:1-13)

Here Jesus warns against the foolishness of not being ready. For those in the parable it was not a question of gross evil, but rather negligence. To neglect Christ will bring destruction in the end as well.

3. Parable of the talents (25:14-30)

Here the warning is for those who are in the kingdom but who fail to expand its borders and fail to serve the king with zeal. This slave was not caught or surprised unprepared, he just assumed that his preparation was sufficient when it was not.

All three parables have the element of preparation, judgment and punishment for those who neglect to prepare for the return of the Master.

Judgment Scene (25:31-46)

The climax of the discourse is the judgment scene at the end of the world. Those found to be righteous have obeyed the commands to love God (they refer to Him as Lord) as well as their neighbor. Those condemned have the same judgment and are condemned because they did not love their neighbor.

The punishment and reward are eternal in nature, a view that is often disturbing to many.

CHAPTER 18
PAUL DESCRIBES THE END

In the New Testament Jesus provides teaching about His second coming in Matthew 24-25, which we covered in the last chapter. He also mentions the end of the Jewish nation in Mark and has several warnings about being prepared for His return in Luke and John, mostly in the form of parables and prayer.

Peter refers to the end times briefly in Acts (3:19-21) and in his letters. In one long passage (II Peter 3:3-13) Peter warns of the suddenness and finality of the events when Jesus returns. Peter also adds the manner in which the world will be destroyed (intense heat), and finishes with a warning to be ready.

There are also brief mentions of the end times in the epistles of Hebrews and James as well as in the Book of Revelation. In Revelation, John the Apostle deals mostly with the plight of the early church under the persecution of Rome and describes his vision of the heavenly realm after the end of the world, but does not provide any information about what actually happens at that historical moment when Jesus returns and the world, as we know it, ends. This task is left to Paul the Apostle who refers to the end of the world and Jesus' return in 9 of his 13 epistles.

I would like to go through these and list the things Paul says about what will happen at the end of the world at Jesus' return.

Romans

> [5] But because of your stubbornness and unrepentant heart you are storing up wrath for yourself in the day of wrath and revelation of the righteous judgment of God, ... [12] For all who have sinned without the Law will also perish without the Law, and all who have sinned under the Law will be judged by the Law; [13] for it is not the hearers of the Law who are just before God, but the doers of the Law will be justified. [14] For when Gentiles who do not have the Law do instinctively the things of the Law, these, not having the Law, are a law to themselves, [15] in that they show the work of the Law written in their hearts, their conscience bearing witness and their thoughts alternately accusing or else defending them, [16] on the day when, according to my gospel, God will judge the secrets of men through Christ Jesus.
> - Romans 2:5, 12-16

This will be a time when God will judge and punish.

> And not only this, but also we ourselves, having the first fruits of the Spirit, even we ourselves groan within ourselves, waiting eagerly for our adoption as sons, the redemption of our body.

> - Romans 8:23

At this time our bodies will be redeemed, meaning that we will be resurrected.

> [10] But you, why do you judge your brother? Or you again, why do you regard your brother with contempt? For we will all stand before the judgment seat of God. [11] For it is written,
> "As I live, says the Lord, every knee shall bow to Me,
> And every tongue shall give praise to God."
> [12] So then each one of us will give an account of himself to God.
> - Romans 14:10-12

Each person will have to give an account to God.

I Corinthians

> who will also confirm you to the end, blameless in the day of our Lord Jesus Christ.
> - I Corinthians 1:8

Jesus will come for His own.

> I have decided to deliver such a one to Satan for the destruction of his flesh, so that his spirit may be saved in the day of the Lord Jesus.
> - I Corinthians 5:5

It will be a day for destruction or salvation depending on our lives lived in faith or not.

23 But each in his own order: Christ the first fruits, after that those who are Christ's at His coming, 24 then comes the end, when He hands over the kingdom to the God and Father, when He has abolished all rule and all authority and power. 25 For He must reign until He has put all His enemies under His feet. 26 The last enemy that will be abolished is death. 27 For He has put all things in subjection under His feet. But when He says, "All things are put in subjection," it is evident that He is excepted who put all things in subjection to Him. 28 When all things are subjected to Him, then the Son Himself also will be subjected to the One who subjected all things to Him, so that God may be all in all.
- I Corinthians 15:23-28

All beings will be in their proper place with perfect unity reestablished between God and man forever.

51 Behold, I tell you a mystery; we will not all sleep, but we will all be changed, 52 in a moment, in the twinkling of an eye, at the last trumpet; for the trumpet will sound, and the dead will be raised imperishable, and we will be changed. 53 For this perishable must put on the imperishable, and this mortal must put on immortality. 54 But when this perishable will have put on the imperishable, and this mortal will have put on immortality, then will come about the saying that is written, "Death is swallowed up in victory.
- I Corinthians 15:51-54

All the events (resurrection, glorification of the saints, punishment of the wicked, destruction of the old and creation of the new world) will happen in the blink of an eye.

II Corinthians

> [1] For we know that if the earthly tent which is our house is torn down, we have a building from God, a house not made with hands, eternal in the heavens.
> [2] For indeed in this house we groan, longing to be clothed with our dwelling from heaven,
> - II Corinthians 5:1-2

The Holy Spirit working in us now gives us an idea of what it will be like when we will have glorified bodies at the return of Jesus.

> For we must all appear before the judgment seat of Christ, so that each one may be recompensed for his deeds in the body, according to what he has done, whether good or bad.
> - II Corinthians 5:10

We will be judged for our deeds.

Philippians

> who will transform the body of our humble state into conformity with the body of His glory, by the exertion of the power that He has even to subject all things to Himself.
> - Philippians 3:21

I Thessalonians

[11] Now may our God and Father Himself and Jesus our Lord direct our way to you; [12] and may the Lord cause you to increase and abound in love for one another, and for all people, just as we also do for you; [13] so that He may establish your hearts without blame in holiness before our God and Father at the coming of our Lord Jesus with all His saints.
- I Thessalonians 3:11-13

The minister's task is to prepare the church to have a loving heart for the return of Jesus.

For you yourselves know full well that the day of the Lord will come just like a thief in the night.
- I Thessalonians 5:2

The return of Jesus will be completely unexpected.

[13] But we do not want you to be uninformed, brethren, about those who are asleep, so that you will not grieve as do the rest who have no hope. [14] For if we believe that Jesus died and rose again, even so God will bring with Him those who have fallen asleep in Jesus. [15] For this we say to you by the word of the Lord, that we who are alive and remain until the coming of the Lord, will not precede those who have fallen asleep. [16] For the Lord Himself will descend from heaven with a shout, with the voice of the archangel and with the trumpet of God, and the dead in Christ will rise first.

[17] Then we who are alive and remain will be

caught up together with them in the clouds to
meet the Lord in the air, and so we shall always
be with the Lord.
- I Thessalonians 4:13-17

When Jesus comes: the dead in Christ will resurrect
first, the faithful who are alive when He comes will join
the resurrected ones, both will be transformed and be
with Christ in the new heavens and earth. Note that
neither Jesus nor the saints are on the earth, no "1000-
year reign" here. Once Jesus appears it is the end of
the old (wicked and unbelieving punished, world
destroyed, new heaven and earth established with God,
Christ, Spirit, saints united; and all of it happens in the
blink of an eye).

[1] Now as to the times and the epochs, brethren,
you have no need of anything to be written to you.
[2] For you yourselves know full well that the day of
the Lord will come just like a thief in the night.
[3] While they are saying, "Peace and safety!" then
destruction will come upon them suddenly like
labor pains upon a woman with child, and they will
not escape.
- I Thessalonians 5:1-3

All of this will happen without signs or warnings.
Actually, the only warning given is to be ready at all
times because you will not see it coming.

II Thessalonians

[7] and to give relief to you who are afflicted and to
us as well when the Lord Jesus will be revealed
from heaven with His mighty angels in flaming

fire, [8] dealing out retribution to those who do not know God and to those who do not obey the gospel of our Lord Jesus.

[9] These will pay the penalty of eternal destruction, away from the presence of the Lord and from the glory of His power, [10] when He comes to be glorified in His saints on that day, and to be marveled at among all who have believed—for our testimony to you was believed.
- II Thessalonians 1:7-10

Those who do not believe will know why they are being punished and those who have been faithful will enjoy the fact that their faith will finally be justified and rewarded.

I Timothy

[14] that you keep the commandment without stain or reproach until the appearing of our Lord Jesus Christ, [15] which He will bring about at the proper time—He who is the blessed and only Sovereign, the King of kings and Lord of lords,
- I Timothy 6:14-15

Jesus will actually appear in real (historical) time, not just a vision. His return is not a spiritual metaphor; at the right time (day/hour/second) He will appear to those alive at that time.

II Timothy

> [1] I solemnly charge you in the presence of God and of Christ Jesus, who is to judge the living and the dead, and by His appearing and His kingdom:
>
> [8] in the future there is laid up for me the crown of righteousness, which the Lord, the righteous Judge, will award to me on that day; and not only to me, but also to all who have loved His appearing.
> - II Timothy 4:1, 8

The coming of Christ will not only bring an end to this world and punishment to the unbelieving and wicked, but also a great reward for the faithful.

Titus

> [11] For the grace of God has appeared, bringing salvation to all men, [12] instructing us to deny ungodliness and worldly desires and to live sensibly, righteously and godly in the present age, [13] looking for the blessed hope and the appearing of the glory of our great God and Savior, Christ Jesus,
> - Titus 2:11-13

We prepare for His sure return by living godly lives now. The more godly our lives, the greater hope we have and joy we will have when He appears.

CHAPTER 19
SUMMARY OF MILLENNIAL THEORIES

As we close out this section on the Second Coming of Christ, here are some final thoughts about the many teachings concerning this important but sometimes difficult subject to understand.

There are four main views / teachings / doctrines concerning the return of Jesus:

Dispensational Premillennialism

People who hold to this idea believe in the "literal" interpretation of the prophetic passages concerning the end times.

Features of this position:

- An actual 1000-year reign of Christ on the earth.

- Two dispensations: one for the salvation of the Jews, then one for the Gentiles.

✓ • A "rapture" where people actually disappear into heaven leaving others on earth.

- The millennium on earth marked by a return of Jewish temple worship, a great war, etc.

Proponents of this teaching:

- Scofield Reference Bible

- Ryrie Study Bible Notes

- Hal Lindsey (The Late, Great Planet Earth)

- Dallas Theological Seminary

- "Left Behind" movies

- Evangelical and charismatic churches

Much of their preaching and teaching revolve around these ideas.

Historic Premillennialism

This position teaches that when Jesus returns He will establish a millennial (1000 years) between the first resurrection and the second resurrection. The final judgment will come at the second resurrection after 1000 years.

Features of this position:

- A great apostasy and tribulation must happen before Jesus returns.

- The kingdom will be revealed and Satan bound during an earthly 1000-year reign.

- A massive rebellion will take place before Jesus returns a second time for judgment.

Proponents of this teaching:

- Fuller Theological Seminary

- George E. Ladd (A Commentary on the Revelation of John)

Post-Millennialism

Post-Millennial scholars believe that the "Millennial Age" begins gradually as the gospel is preached. The church exercises its authority in financial and political ways on the earth as a sign of the supremacy of the "kingdom."

Features of this position:

- The church "binds" Satan and his influence on the earth.

- Proponents believe in a form of Christian theocracy.

Proponents of this teaching:

- Charles Hodge
- B.B. Warfield
- Kenneth Copeland
- Pat Robertson

A-Millennialism

Those who hold this position teach that the 1000 years refers to the time between Jesus' initial appearance and

His second and final return at the end of the world. This number is not literally 1000 years but a symbolic time frame, the length of which only known by God.

Jesus established the kingdom on earth when He came and the kingdom grows through the preaching of the gospel until His return.

Features of this position:

- No rapture/tribulation, etc.

- Both Jews and Gentiles are called into the kingdom by the same gospel.

- The kingdom is represented by the church on the earth.

- At Jesus' return the world will end, the wicked will be judged, the saints will be with Christ in the new heaven and earth forever.

Proponents of this teaching:

- Majority position of Christianity in general
- J. I. Packard
- R.C. Sproul
- Stafford North
- Churches of Christ
- *Expanded notes available at: bibletalk.tv/eschatology-chart*

In closing please know that my sincere prayer is that after reading this book you will have a better understanding of the Christian religion, and your faith will have been strengthened with the knowledge gained.

Mike Mazzalongo
Oklahoma City
May 25, 2016

BibleTalk.tv is an Internet Mission Work.

We provide textual Bible teaching material on our website and mobile apps for free. We enable churches and individuals all over the world to have access to sound Bible teaching resources.

The goal of this mission work is to spread the gospel to the greatest number of people using the latest technology available. For the first time in history it is becoming possible to preach the gospel to the entire world at once. BibleTalk.tv is an effort to preach the gospel to all nations every day until Jesus returns.

The Choctaw Church of Christ in Oklahoma City is the sponsoring congregation for this work and provides the oversight for the BibleTalk ministry team. If you would like information on how you can support this ministry, please go to the link provided below.

bibletalk.tv/support

Made in the USA
San Bernardino, CA
31 October 2016